When life handed ~~these~~
Teachers turned them into Lemonade!

The Lemonade Series

Teaching with Love, Laughter & Lemonade

By Paul S. Bodner

Award Winning Stories about Teachers who have changed a student's life, written by their own students, in their own words!

Appreciate those who care…and care for those you appreciate!

Dad's Lemonade Stand

Tips on Living with Love, Laughter and Lemonade!

The stories in this book have been written by high
school students as part of a scholarship program sponsored by
"The Lemonade Series."

Library of Congress Cataloging-in-Publication Date

Copyrighted in the United States 2003. Printed in the United
States of America. Except as permitted under the Copyright Act of
1976, no part of this publication may be reproduced or distributed in
any form or by any means, or stored in any database or electronic
retrieval system without express written permission of the publisher.

Published by Dad's Lemonade Stand, Inc.
Las Vegas, Nevada

Purchase of additional copies or bulk purchase requests may be
made by contacting the publisher at (702) 579-7230, or on the
Internet at: www.DadsLemonadeStand.com

First Edition 2003

Dedication

To Mrs. Demarest, and to all my teachers in Longfellow, Hawthorne and Teaneck High school. Thank you to the world of teachers, who commit their lives to helping the rest of us find our way.

It's only when you peel back its skin, that you discover the real essence of the lemon.

Dad's Lemonade Stand

Tips on Living with Love, Laughter and Lemonade!

Acknowledgements

Teachers feed our minds, preparing us to live our lives to better the world. To this end, there is no more noble a profession. And so we say, thank you.

Special thanks to:

My wife, Ellen, for being my life long partner & soul mate;

My children, Zack and Gabe, for filling my heart with pride;

My dear friends, who served on the Editorial Board:

> Bob Benedetto, Educator and Screenwriter
> Ira Blumenthal, Professor, Author, Speaker
> Ellen Bodner, Wife, Mother, Professional Designer
> Deborah Ettinger, Health Care Executive, Writer
> Lucie Hinden, Teacher – Beverly Hills High School, CA
> Brenda Hirsch, Teacher – Raul P. Elizondo Elem. School, Las Vegas, Nevada
> Phillip Nobert, Creative Director, Advertising Executive
> Marcia Sainer, Retired Editor, Active Mom
> Jack Singer, PhD – Psychologist, Speaker, Writer
> Phyllis Vajda – Executive Search Professional, Retired Teacher

My Co-Editor – Annie Flanzraich. Annie is now a freshman at UNR, where she is studying journalism. It was through her eyes that I saw our authors' point of view. It was also through her heart, that I heard our authors' voices. Thank you, Annie

My partner – Fred Marks. Fred has been the wind beneath my wings from concept to creation. His genuine friendship and honest feedback have made this project a labor of love. Thank you, Fred.

My "Lemonade" team:

> Jim Severson – Illustrator Extraordinaire
> John Main – Amazing Graphic Designer
> Sandy Fermahin – Primo Executive Assistant
> Shirley Wolf – Top Typist
> Rod Buckle – Cover Photography

Foreword

"This book is for you," she said, as she paid the worker at my 5th grade book fair, handing me, "The Mickey Mantle Story." I read this book cover to cover, many times over, but more than that, this gesture of kindness opened up my world to a life of reading, and ultimately, writing.

But, I'm getting ahead of myself. Allow me to catch you up, and fill you in on how this experience changed my love of reading, and how this teacher led me to write this book, "Teaching with Love & Laughter."

Several years ago, I was visiting my son Zack, on a trip to Connecticut. I stayed in a bed and breakfast inn, enjoying the beauty of the countryside, and the fun of meeting new people. As I was introducing myself to the other travelers over breakfast, the usual background bits and pieces of our lives were being shared:

"Where you from?" I asked a lovely retired couple who were antiquing in New England.

"A small town in North Jersey," they responded.

"So am I," I said. "What town?"

"Teaneck. Do you know it?"

"That's where I'm from!" I said, as the conversation became more focused on this piece of news.

This sweet, blue eyed lady looked at me with amazement.

"Really, that's quite a coincidence. What school did you go to?"

I looked at her, and smiled, "There was only one high school, Teaneck High School."

"I know that," she responded, with her eyes twinkling, "I meant what grammar school?"

"Actually, it was Hawthorne Elementary."

And before I could say another word, she reached over and grabbed her husband's arm, and said, "Who was your fifth grade teacher?"

Now the room was entirely quiet, listening to our conversation. I did not hesitate for a moment as I said, "Mrs. Demarest...one of the most incredible teachers in the world!"

This kind and gentle couple held each other's hands tightly, as she turned to me with tears in her eyes, and quietly said, "I'm Mrs. Demarest."

You could have heard the leaves changing colors, it had turned so quiet.

"Really??? Well, that is so amazing!" I turned to both of them, and continued, "I always wanted to tell you, Mrs. Demarest, how important you were to me."

She was listening to every word with interest.

"In fifth grade, you took me to the book fair, and, knowing that I did not have enough money to buy the one book that I really wanted, you reached in your own wallet and bought me, 'The Mickey Mantle Story.' That book turned me on to reading and writing, and literally changed my world. It was all due to your kindness, and I always wanted to thank you, and let you know how positively you changed my life."

Well, now, she started crying, and her husband was crying, and everyone in the room started crying. But then they all started talking about teachers who changed their lives…and I came back home and every one I told this story to, also told me about a teacher in their lives. And so, this book was born!

I am most grateful for all the wonderful stories that have been submitted from people throughout the world, and I look forward to continuing to publish these stories, all with the hope that the teachers who have been so significant in so many lives can truly know how appreciated they are!

With love and laughter,
Paul S. Bodner

Table Of Contents

Beyond A Requiem—Britt Flaherty 1

A Valuable Lesson In Life—Samara Abbott 3

Sergeant Major—Skye Andrade 4

You Want Me On Your Résumé—Anthony Angiuli 6

Through The Eyes Of A Fourth Grader—Laura Arnold 8

Lighting Up The Whiteboard—Alea Arquines 10

Teaching With Love And Laughter—Joshua Artz 12

The Influences Of A Great Man—Rahul Bansal 14

The Nine Week Awakening—Kellie Beck 16

My Teacher Ate My Homework—Kelly Blosser 17

Grandpa Roma—Nadya Bronstein 18

What I Didn't Learn From A Book—Kayla Brooks 20

The Music Of My Life—Joseph Bryant 22

My Teacher Is My Mom—Katie Bryant 24

Commit Without Hesitancy—John Butcher 26

He Welded My Career—David Cable 27

Mr. Breslin, A Brilliant Man—Miranda Church 29

Eckart Chemistry—Crystal Cleveland 30

She Changed My Life—Becci Clippinger 32

Importance Of Interpretation—Camille Cohen 34

Inspiration At A Glance—Jessica Collier 36

Bring On The Sharks—Lauren Connolly 38

I Would Die For You—Kyndra Connor 40

Real Music—Bethany Corriveau 42

A Hero—Claudia Dimanche 44

Major Hall's Chosen Few—Katherine Dozer 46

My Teacher My Friend—Frankie Eskridge 48

Teaching With Love And Laughter—Debra Evans 50

A Teacher's Big Impact—Kristen Ford 52

The Most Important Lesson—Blake French 54

Important Lessons In Life And Music—Lauren Gage 56

Connecting Beneath The Skin—Caroline Gagola 58

He Saved My Life—Megan Goracke 59

A Teacher & Friend—James Greco 60

He Never Gave Up—Aaron Grove 62

My Second Grade Teacher—Ashley Harter 64

My Teacher, My Friend—Megan Havens 65

The True Meaning Of Teaching—Rachel Henrich 67

Last Names And Simple Abundances—Kelli Hogan 69

Write Now—Victoria Hughes 71

The Who, What And Where Of My "Special" Education—

    Michael Hurt 73

The Lasting Ripple—Kelly Iwanabe 75

Friendship Through Music—Danielle Jefferis 77

In The Making—Jamie Jetton 79

Learn How You Are Not Stupid, But If You Keep It Up,

    You Will Be—Corie Kellman 81

How One Teacher Influenced My Life—Aimee Kidd 83

What It Means To Be A Teacher—Kathryn Kleohn 85

I Learned How To Go On—Melissa Knutson 87

Realizing Through Hardship—Ryan Lassabe 89

A Breath Of Fresh Air—Catherine Lawhon 91

Kindred Spirit—Jessica Liptak 93

My Favorite Pair Of Underwear—Keane Maddock 95

Brick By Brick—Erin Marcoe 97

Ode To Mrs. Renee Buchholz—Barry Marquardt 99

The Inspiration To Think For Myself—Melissa Marrero 101

The Voice Of Love—Lashanna Martin 103

My Motivation—Shaday Matthews 105

The World's Kindest Teacher—Elizabeth McIlwain 107

An Unknown Blessing—Jasmin Mercedes 108

Lesson Of Life—Tanya Methven 109

Uncle Pete—Megan Minkow 111

The Teacher Who Never Leaves My Side—Christina Molino 113

Daddy I Found You—Grace Monrian 115

He Believes In Me—Cherry Mun 117

Accent On Success—Doris Oghor 119

Mr. Mooney—Erin Olshever 121

Care Spelled, Carr—Roxanne Parker 123

His Eyes Twinkled With Care—Betsy Potter 125

The Teacher Who Inspired Me To Change My Life—
    Eric Pouliot 127

Kind Words And A Gentle Heart—Jenni Rainey 129

The Story Of Jessica—Jessica Reeder 131

The Teacher Who Taught Me To Make Lemonade From Lemons—
    Cynthia Roth 133

A Wonderful Ride Through Life—Leah San Agustin 135

Remind Me—Kathryn Semple 137

Mrs. Thomas—Misty Snyder 139

I Have Succeeded—Gretchen Soto 141

You Amaze Me—Allison Speicher 142

Don't Rush—Shayla Stanley 144

Forever Happy, Forever Grateful—Karen Stufflebeam 145

Teaching With Love And Laughter—Whitney Sugg 147

Mr. Cwodzinski—Anna-Lisa Swank 149

Mr. Coward's Gumballs—Leslie Tharp 151

Teaching With Love And Laughter—Mary Tolson 153

The Greatest Teacher—Katelyn Twichell 155

A Lucrative Education—Kate Vershov 157

An Epiphany Of Empathy—Judith Vick 159

One Little Speech—Candace Vickers 161

The Magister—Aaron Warchal 163

My Teacher; My Savior—Jessica Rose Weiner 165

"Dukey"—Ashley Wetherell 166

Lemon Jelly—Bridget Williams 168

Sweetener Of My Lemonade—Liynaa'a Willoughby 169

Name, Dates, And Friendship—David Wonpu 170

The Unforgettable Mr. Ron Carr—Adam Zaremba 172

English As A Second Language—Elena Zeltser 174

The Path—Joyce Zhang 176

Beyond A Requiem

by Britt Flaherty

I arrived at Idyllwild Arts Camp at the tail end of the summer after my sophomore year. Stepping into the large auditorium, I was given a small booklet entitled Mozart's Requiem, and I skimmed the pages briefly. I was to spend two weeks rehearsing this piece, studying both its origins and musicality. However, I did not know at the time that in these two weeks, I was to realize how great of an influence music may have on a person and on her attitude towards life.

The choral instructor was Mrs. Bielefeld, a woman in her elder years who I soon realized was at the end of a long battle with cancer. Despite an oxygen tank and incredible physical disabilities, she was proud enough to throw her straw hat off of her bald head and announce that today, we would really learn how to make music; and that we did. In two weeks, my musical capabilities exploded. I learned more about technique than ever before. However, what I really learned was how to feel the incredible melody Mozart had written years before, as he felt death approaching. Mrs. Bielefeld held intensive small group sessions to learn the music, and large group talks to discuss its meaning. The altos once asked why there was such a great tone change between the dark and haunting section, "Domine Jesu," and the cheerful and praising tune of "Hostias." She explained that the road to death can lead us first to fear, and then to exultation at the time we have been allowed to live. She also showed her strength when, as her sickness progressed, she pushed the choir to work its hardest and make the best out of the small time she would spend with us.

Maybe it was because the woman in front of me was going through the process I was singing about: maybe it was because I studied the Requiem's origins for days before the performance. Whatever the reason, when I stood on the stage the last Saturday at camp, I became completely enthralled with the music. I wept for the beauty and sadness the requiem expressed, and I sang with the emotion Mrs. Bielefeld had so often preached about. As I watched her

The Lemonade Series

conduct, I saw that this performance would likely be her last. It was on that day that I realized how Mrs. Bielefeld, and anyone who truly loved music, used it not only as a pastime, but also as a release. Music could be used to embody emotions not so easily expressed with words.

I received a phone call a few weeks after camp telling me that Mrs. Bielefeld had passed away. Her ability to smile in the face of death will forever inspire me to see good things that are left when times are rough. She taught me to use music as a means of expression for unspoken emotions. Mrs. Bielefeld touched my life for a brief moment, but her impact will last forever.

A Valuable Lesson In Life
by Samara Abbott

My first year of high school, I was fortunate enough to have Mr. Dreyer as my history teacher. Not only is he an incredibly knowledgeable teacher, but he is also a genuinely good person. Having him as a teacher completely changed the attitude I have for my future.

Every one knows that he rides his bicycle to school many mornings, but we assumed that it was for economical reasons. One day he told my class about how he rides his bicycle to school instead of driving his car because it gave him the opportunity to wave to his neighbors and greet children waiting at the bus stop. He said that if he were driving to school, he probably would not notice the people outside in the morning or afternoons, let alone have the chance to say hello.

This taught me a valuable lesson. Before Mr. Dreyer told my class this story, I had always defined success as eventually having a job that made a lot of money. This teacher made me realize that in life, money is not always the one-way street to happiness. Mr. Dreyer taught me to value the relationships I have with other people rather than monetary items. More importantly, he taught me to slow down and enjoy life. Just like he did not want to speed by his neighbors, he made me realize that I do not want to speed by things in my life and take them for granted.

What a great way to start each day! A wave and a smile... What else do you need to be happy?!

Whenever things start to get hectic, I remember that making convenience a top priority is not always the best thing to do. Whenever I think about what I do not have, I think about Mr. Dreyer riding his bike to school and realize that everything around me is all I really need.

The Lemonade Series

Sergeant Major
by Skye Andrade

When I had entered the seventh grade I was a loner. I wasn't popular. I didn't have many friends; I was a "nerd." By the end of my seventh-grade year, I had made up my mind that things would change. My life would change, I would change.

During my first few days of the eight-grade, I started hanging out with an old friend I had known in elementary. She, unlike myself, had been adopted into the "popular" world because of her good looks and outgoing personality. She also had a high school boyfriend and high school friends.

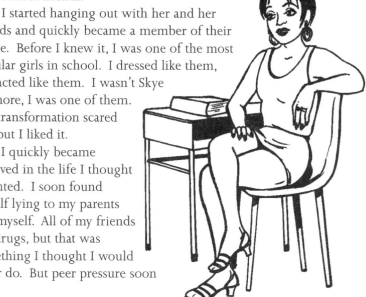

I dress like them, look like them, Act like them…but something's still missing!

I started hanging out with her and her friends and quickly became a member of their clique. Before I knew it, I was one of the most popular girls in school. I dressed like them, and acted like them. I wasn't Skye anymore, I was one of them. The transformation scared me, but I liked it.

I quickly became involved in the life I thought I wanted. I soon found myself lying to my parents and myself. All of my friends did drugs, but that was something I thought I would never do. But peer pressure soon took its toll. My friends drank and smoked pot, and so did I. My friends were having sex, and so was I.

That year my grades fell and my personality changed. I was no longer the "good student" teachers liked; I was the "problem child" teachers feared. My parents could no longer brag about me with pride, instead I was a disappointment with bad grades, dark lipstick and short skirts.

When I entered my freshman year, things were the same, same friends, same lifestyle. But I had done something different than my friends. I had signed up for the J.R.O.T.C. program. My instructor was a man named Sgt. Maj. Nago. He would soon change my life.

Sgt. Maj. was a retired Army man. He took so much pride in everything he did. He loved teaching. He taught me to have pride in myself. He showed me that you shouldn't be the person people want you to be, you had to be who you wanted to be. When I wanted to give up he always said, "I'll give you a key and a straw, so suck it up and drive on!"

I soon excelled in the program and ditched my old friends. One day Sgt. Maj. told me that if I keep doing what I'm doing, I would be our school's first female Battalion Commander. Those words inspired me. If he believed I could do it, then I knew I could. When he retired, I was a junior. I was determined not to fail him.

Today I am Cadet Lt. Col., Battalion commander. My old friends either dropped out or are pregnant. In June, I will be attending Embry-Riddle Aeronautical University to become a pilot. I take pride in myself and everything I do, and I have Sgt. Maj. Nago to thank. Thank you Sgt. Maj.

The Lemonade Series

You Want Me On Your Resume
by Anthony Angiuli

About a year and a half ago, I thought I was doing just fine. I was receiving top honors, enjoying varsity sports, and participating in various community projects. All looked positive except for the fact that I was feeling quite average. Something was missing in my life and it nagged at me continuously. How was I ever going to rise above and stand out from the huge applicant pool of high school kids? After joining the most active club on campus, the Key Club, I began to feel an amazing change. My religion teacher, Ms. Cathy Lewis, was rambling on about community service ideas. I kept hearing her southern drawl in my head and her exceedingly lengthy monologue. The intensity at which she taught was overwhelming, but she stuck to you like glue. I couldn't shake her!

One day she noticed my activity level at the Key Club and said words to me that changed my attitude and my life. She raised the bar for me. "You will want me on your college resume," is what she said. That hit me like a ton of bricks. I began to sit up in class, pay more attention and actually learn to love her southern inflection. She was teaching "Morals and Ethics" and everything began to click. After all my efforts in 10th grade, I was awarded the school's Community Service Award. Wow, how did this happen, and especially to me? This was something I realized that I was good at. Ms. Lewis began to compliment me more, encourage me more, and ask for my help in various projects. She actually made me feel important and told me that I had leadership qualities. No one had ever said this to me before. Even some of my friends were noticing a change in me. For my junior year I initiated many projects and became the Key Club Treasurer. I have been encouraged by Ms. Lewis to try and win the Distinguished Key Club Treasurer Award.

Because of the accomplishments and volunteer programs that the Key Club participates in, Ms. Lewis won county recognition for winning the "Teacher That Makes a Difference Award." Her selfless hours spent for the betterment of her students and surrounding community are overwhelming. Watching an adult continue her love of guiding others has made a huge impact on me and even raised the echelon of colleges that I thought I could get into. This level of confidence that she has placed in me has inspired me to stretch both personally and academically. Thanks to this loving and generous teacher I am on a brighter path to my future. She still has that twang in her voice and still leaves extremely long messages on the recorder that make me chuckle, but now I listen to them with deep fondness and appreciation. Thank you, Cathy Lewis.

Through The Eyes Of A Fourth Grader

by Laura Arnold

The fourth grade classroom was daunting. The first day of school had arrived, much to my disappointment, and to make matters worse we had assigned seats right off the bat. I found my nametag, and sat down sulking. After a few of the longest minutes in my life, Cynthia came in and took the seat across from me. Cynthia was a walking target to the rest of the fourth grade class. Her hair was knotted and her clothes were often torn. She was the kid that no one would talk to, and now I had to sit with her.

Everyday with Ms. Groff at the head of the class attempting to instruct, Cynthia would yell out random comments that would disrupt the class. Unprovoked, she would kick my shins under the desk and occasionally throw pencils in my direction. Without warning she would begin yelling or physically lash out towards Ms. Goff. Once, I remember her standing with a chair above her head threatening the

> Go ahead, dear, get it out of your system...Inside you is a beautiful flower...Waiting to bloom!

teacher. When we did group work at our desk, Ms. Goff would have to come over and give us separate instructions and try to prompt Cynthia to attempt the task. Cynthia's responses ranged from spitting to yelling to throwing objects, and all the while Ms. Gruff would stand there and wait until the student had finished, then try to redirect her energy.

After the end of the first quarter everyone was assigned new seats, but Cynthia and I still sat together; Ms. Groff had tried to explain to me why my seat had not changed, but the mentality of a fourth grader would not comprehend the meaning behind her explanation. The weeks dragged by, and her behavior continued as usual, although sometimes there were reprieves where we could function like the other groups. At the height of her problems, I remember Cynthia being physically removed from the classroom after a severe temper-tantrum. I remember Ms. Goff standing before the class stumbling to find the words that would explain why our peer had just been carried from the classroom kicking and screaming. With twenty-four sets of inquisitive eyes staring at her and with tears streaming from her eyes, Ms. Goff tried to explain that Cynthia was sick and had to go to another school that would be able to help her. Ms. Groff had filled a basket with books and candies and encouraged us to sign a card, all of which would be taken to Cynthia. I recall sitting there in bewilderment after everything Cynthia had done to Ms. Groff, yet Ms. Groff was upset to see her leave.

It was not until years later that I could fully grasp what had taken place in the fourth grade classroom. The image of a woman expressing sheer compassion towards someone that enacted the cruelest of conduct has stuck with me for several years now. It taught me an irreplaceable lesson in tolerance, forgiveness, and empathy.

Lighting Up The Whiteboard

by Alea Arquines

I'm sure everyone has heard of the stereotype of the teacher who is a grumpy old man or woman, who hates kids, but needs the money for retirement. Or even worse, to pay off student loans from who knows how many years ago. For many years, I thought it was true. I consider myself lucky to have one teacher who completely defied that stereotype.

He's a graduate from Princeton University, and somehow, he ended up working as a math teacher at Sammamish High School in small town Bellevue, WA. For years, I hated math because I thought it was too boring and too hard to grasp. Mr. Goldstein is one of those teachers who makes you say on the 1st day of class, "This is going to be an interesting year." At first, you really don't know if interesting is going to be good or bad.

It's a blank board now,
But think of the possibilities!

Teaching with Love, Laughter & Lemonade

I had math 1st period at 7:30 am. Not only do I hate math at this point, but I'm also experiencing morning grumpiness. I enter the class with a wobble and a face only a mother could love. He takes one look at me and laughs with complete understanding. And then— a smile leaks out of me unexpectedly! Darn! When the bell rings, I sit at my desk, obstinate, knowing that I won't learn a dang thing. No other math teacher has ever taught me anything that I could remember, why would junior year be any different? Bit it is. Everyday, there he is in front of class, hyper and enthusiastic to teach. Can you help not smiling and laughing when there's a teacher who lights up the classroom with positive enthusiasm and who makes the numbers on the whiteboard come to life in sprightly dance?

Sometimes, he made me guilty when I was being grumpy. He is so young and he jumps around like he's a 5 year old overdosing on sugar cubes. His happiness about working with math is overwhelmingly contagious to his students. Because of Mr. Goldstein, I love math. With him, there was never a stupid question. In an Honors Junior level of math, he was always patient even with questions such as, why does a positive number multiplied by a negative number equal a negative number? This was a class where learning flourished.

Everyday, I woke up to a class like this. I certainly didn't have the highest grade but I did manage to keep a strong A going. Unlike other math teachers, he didn't believe in having his students memorize formulas and figures. He wanted us to learn to use our heads and know where those formulas come from. Even when the course was over, he was happy to help me with SAT math questions before school started.

Teaching is his life—his love. Ask him what his passion is and he'll say, "Math makes me abandon my morals!" School would be endless depression if not for teachers like Mr. Goldstein.

Teaching With Love And Laughter

by Joshua Artz

My name is Josh Artz, I am eighteen years old and I go to Germantown High School. I live with my mom and dad, my two brothers and my sister. I have not always lived with the family that I have right now. When I was in elementary school, I attended several different schools because of my biological dad's job. We moved back and forth from Arkansas to Memphis several times. I attended one school in Arkansas for six days. When I was in the fourth grade, I was attending Grahamwood Elementary School here in Memphis, TN. My fourth grade teacher's name was Mrs. Peepers. She had just gotten married that year. I remember her husband coming to see her at school, and I, along with the rest of the students, thought he was a pretty cool guy. Toward the end of the year, something happened to me that caused Mrs. Peepers to become not only my teacher, but my friend.

One Wednesday after my family came home from church, my mom was killed. After we pulled into the driveway of our house, my mom opened the door and was shot several times in the head. My two brothers and I were in the car, so when I finally realized what had happened I ran to a neighbor's house and they called 911. My mom died instantly. For a long time it was really hard to talk to anyone about what I had seen that night. I remember talking to a friend, my grandmother, and my fourth grade teacher, Mrs. Peepers. Mrs. Peepers went out of her way to make sure that she could do anything she could for me. I remember her coming over and talking to my grandmother and me, and thinking that it was weird to have my teacher spend her time outside of school with me. I also remember Mrs. Peepers buying books for me out of the Scholastic Book Orders, and now when I look back on what she did for me, I see how special it was and how much it meant to me. She helped me get back into the flow of school very easily and quickly.

Just recently I saw Mrs. Peepers at a Redbirds baseball game, and I had the chance to thank her for all that she had done for me. When

I was going through that hard time after losing my mom, I see now that Mrs. Peepers was my teacher and I respect her for that, but she also became my friend.

I'm adopted and live with my two biological brothers and my sister who is also adopted. I attend Central Church and am involved with youth. I stay very busy. As of right now, my plans are to attend John Brown University in Siloam Springs, AR, and if I win this scholarship, it will be an answer to a prayer for the funds for college this fall.

The Influences Of A Great Man

by Rahul Bansal

There have been countless people in my life who have taught me useful knowledge about many things. From each of them I learned something new that would serve to better my life in the future. None of these lessons, however, match the influence that my high school band director had on me. Mr. Frank Troyka has taught me an inconceivable amount of knowledge about learning, about competitive drive and remaining humble, and so many more topics. I am entirely grateful for the magnitude by which Mr. Troyka has improved my life.

> He taught me more than the key of C—
> He taught me the keys to success!

I met Mr. Troyka on day one of 10th grade and immediately the learning process began. He taught me the four keys to success in band, which are ultimately the four keys to success in learning: attendance, attitude, mental ability, and physical ability. He said attendance was the most important because if you're not there then you can't learn. Then a healthy attitude was required because there needed to be some motivation to learn. Third, you needed mental ability to stay concentrated on the task at hand, and ultimately the physical ability would come along as a result. I had known him for one day and

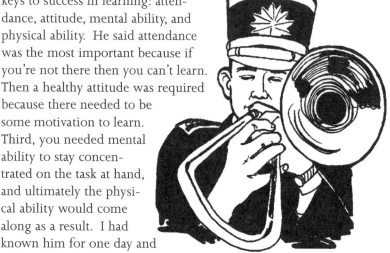

already he had taught me the most effective learning strategy yet. This was merely a start to what would turn into a great relationship.

Mr. Troyka taught me that if you put your mind and heart into a task it can be done. He said that people who say they can fly in their heart truly believe that they can't, so they don't fly. He taught me that "whether you think you can or think you can't you're always right." The attitude for success must be there for success to exist.

He taught me much in the way of competitive drive and remaining humble. Mr. Troyka believed and made me believe that if you're going to do something, put your whole effort into it. When I am asked to raise my hand, it goes all the way up with full extension. When I am asked to hustle, it means running with an objective in mind. These things may seem small, but they enhance competitiveness greatly. Sometimes our band would lose marching contests and we would think that we were cheated. We would get frustrated, ready to bad mouth other bands in public. Mr. Troyka would stop us and teach us humbleness. He would say, "Don't go bad mouthing other bands. Remember that you represent your name, your band, and most importantly, your family." The moral code by which he lives is the example we should all follow.

I will never forget what he has taught me in the three years that I have known him. This past school year, Mr. Troyka received the Teacher of the Year Award among 200+ teachers at our school. The award recipient could not have been chosen any better. Mr. Troyka deserved it then and he deserves it every year as long as he continues teaching.

The Nine Week Awakening
by Kellie Beck

Many teachers have impacted me for the better throughout my high school career, but one teacher has truly stood out as phenomenal. That teacher is Mr. Ben Cox. During my senior year I was fortunate enough to have Mr. Cox as my teacher for nine weeks in a World Religions class. When entering this class I had no idea of what to expect, least of all, that I was in for a life changing experience.

Before this class, I assumed that I knew all I would ever need to know about the religions and cultures around me. I came from a strong Christian background and had the basic opinion that if they weren't Christian they were wrong. Was I ever in for a rude awakening.

Mr. Cox's manner of teaching not only showed you the basics of the religion you were studying, but also the way the people lived and how their religion impacted their day-to-day lives. In only nine weeks, Mr. Cox was able to open my eyes to the necessity of understanding. If we don't understand and appreciate each religion and culture for its own merits, it is impossible for peace and friendship to ever be attained. This is the change that occurred within me.

I will always be grateful to Mr. Cox for teaching the class in his way and showing me the need for acceptance of other ways of life, even if they are not our own. I had never thought that a mere nine weeks could forever change my opinions of my entire lifestyle, and so fully lead me to understand the actions of those around me.

My Teacher Ate My Homework

by Kelly Blosser

Rip, Rip, Rip! Most students would be outraged at having an assignment torn up and thrown in the trash. To me, it was a challenge. Usually, in school I was bored. The work was easy, and I only had to put forth minimal effort. I considered school a waste of time. That is, until I had Mrs. Brown.

Mrs. Brown was my 7th grade English teacher. I had moved to a new school district right before school started, so I wasn't tested to go into any of the harder classes. I found that the classes I was in went over material I had learned years before. It was like repeating a grade, and to me, it appeared to be pointless. I begged my mother to let me stay home, sometimes even crying about not going to school. But I had to go.

After one particularly boring week, my mother decided it was time for a change. She went into the school, and talked to each of my teachers, challenging them to challenge me. Only Mrs. Brown took up the challenge. She pushed me harder than any of her other students, tearing up my work when she thought it wasn't my best, requiring me to put forth more than the just the bare minimum effort. The long, boring day didn't seem as long or as boring when I had English class to look forward to at the end of each day.

Then, to my delight, Mrs. Brown informed me that she was starting a writing club. Meetings would be held every other Thursday after school. I jumped at the opportunity. During those few hours a month, I learned more than I had all year. We worked on poetry and short stories, and we were paired up with high school tutors to improve our papers. When I look back at all the writing I have done, my very best is when I had Mrs. Brown as my teacher.

The Lemonade Series

Grandpa Roma

by Nadya Bronstein

I open the door and see a poorly illuminated room, a shabby sofa, and a shaky dinner table. On the sofa and threadbare quilt sit several children approximately my age, laughing hysterically. Each child holds a hotdog in one hand, a slice of bread in the other. Upon seeing me, they become quiet, and I notice a man resembling Santa Claus, with thick gray hair, shaggy eyebrows, and a kind smile. "Come in Nadya, join us." The children move over, leaving me a corner of the sofa to sit on. The old man immediately hands me a hot dog in a bun. And so my peers and I laugh, eat hotdogs, wait for our moms and dads, and listen to the amazing stories of "Santa Claus" who everyone calls Grandpa Roma.

This picture is imprinted in my childhood memories. I had never experienced as much happiness and peacefulness as in that shabby apartment, and hotdogs had never tasted so delicious. Why had Grandpa Roma entered my life in those three summer months?

In June of 1991, my life turned upside-down. I only recollect that mother was crying, that my father was unusually sad, and that there were three small carry-on bags in our apartment.

Sometimes lemonade comes in a bun.

My mother told me that one of them was mine, and that I should put in only what I could not imagine my life without, because as refugees, we were only allowed one bag per person. She tried to explain to me that we were leaving our country forever. At six years old I did not understand why I had to leave my home, friends, and toys behind. Why were we called refugees? My new life in America was filled with anxiety, loneliness and confusion. But everything changed from the moment I opened the door to Grandpa Roma's apartment.

Grandpa Roma was a refugee like the rest of us, and he was also our kindergarten teacher. About a dozen immigrant families from the former Soviet Union had moved into one apartment complex. Since the Soviet government allowed each family to take only $100 with them, when we arrived in America, the adults were forced to earn money immediately to survive. My parents worked day and night, and went to school to learn English. But what would they do with the children? To our relief, there was Grandpa Roma, who was old and sick, but still had the desire to teach us. The few food stamps he received, he spent on us. His tiny room was a kindergarten, cafeteria, and a home for immigrant children. He did all this for free, without expecting anything in return.

Years passed. My parents and their friends bought houses, moved to other cities. And Grandpa Roma? Grandpa Roma died last year, at the age of eighty-three. The whole Russian community came to the funeral of the man who had spent a fortune on hotdogs for immigrant children throughout the years. He was a poor man with a rich soul.

The Lemonade Series

What I Didn't Learn From A Book

by Kayla Brooks

When I came to Henrietta three years ago, I felt nervous, yet excited. I was a sophomore in a new town, trying to make new friends. I wasn't very popular at my old school, but I suppose it's hard to be popular in a sea of 4,000 faces.

One thing was sure—my face would definitely stand out in this crowd. Everyone wondered who I was because I was new and because I was black. To my surprise, people received me with enthusiasm and a strange curiosity.

With the big move came big changes. I was accustomed to having four classes a day. Now, I had seven classes a day. But that wasn't the hard part. At my school, you had Theatre 1-4, in which you moved up to the next level of theatre with each year. Henrietta was different; you took theatre for one year—and that was it!

This was disappointing to me. I had just gotten into acting, and was finding it to be an excellent outlet for energy and stress. Now, I was in a class learning things I already knew. Luckily for me, I had a teacher who wanted to teach me that being on stage was more than learning lines and getting a laugh.

Mrs. Scott simply picked up where my former teacher had left off. She emphasized what I already knew and taught me things I probably wouldn't have learned anywhere else. She made me laugh and showed me movies that made me cry. I learned to appreciate theatre for more than what it was on the surface. I learned how important the technical side of theatre is and just how "dramatically" I can affect someone else by what I do on stage.

When spring came, I auditioned for a One-Act Play. I was nervous, and it showed because I didn't get a part. Instead of quitting, I agreed to be on the crew and stay committed. As I read in place of another member who was missing practices, Mrs. Scott realized I was more relaxed and natural. When the member had to quit, I replaced her. Mrs. Scott had faith in me, yelled at me when I needed it, and praised me when I deserved it.

I competed that first time and won Best-Actress. It was the proudest moment of my life, and she was right there cheering me on. At that moment, I became sure I wanted to teach theatre. I wanted kids to have the love, respect, and admiration I had for Mrs. Scott.

She was my second mother at times, and I've always been able to depend on her for everything. From recommendation letters, to a pair of pantyhose, she's always been there. I hope someday, when I'm a teacher, or maybe a famous actress, she'll be there watching and waiting to say, "I always knew you could do it. I always knew!"

Begin each day with a hug and a smile.

Dad's Lemonade Stand

Tips on Living with Love, Laughter and Lemonade!

The Music Of My Life

by Joseph Bryant

There have been many teachers who have had a positive influence on me. But there is one teacher that had the most positive influence on me. This teacher was Ms. Virginia Lam. She was the music teacher at John Wanamaker Middle School, in the heart of North Philadelphia. This is where I attended school after attending a private school.

While I was in middle school, I was the subject of a lot of other students' ridicule. I was teased because of several things: the way I dressed—Payless shoes and Bo Bo's, my "bottle-cap" glasses, and the fact that I was further along in my intellectual development than most of the students in my class. This had a negative effect on my self esteem; I would be sad every day because of my hurt feelings.

I was scheduled for music class with Ms. Lam. I enjoyed the class because one, I excelled in it, and two, because it made me feel better and allowed me to release some of my depression. Ms. Lam noticed my plight and befriended me. Our relationship got to the level where we could share our inner feelings about things, such as life. This is when she began to exert her positive influence on me. She told me things about life that I had not yet experienced. Things like jealousy, and envy. From then on, she became my in-school advisor, helping me on an as-needed basis.

Ms. Lam then encouraged me to enter the performing arts group. I joined the group, sometimes touring the city with our repertoire of songs and dances. This allowed Ms. Lam to bring out the real me, and to nurture a potential performing artist. I thoroughly enjoyed performing with the group, and I began to enjoy life and its pleasures.

After two and a half years of performing with the group, I was encouraged by Ms. Lam to audition for the performing arts high school. I took her advice, auditioning as a dance major. I was later astounded to learn that I was accepted into the school. I then thanked Ms. Lam for her help and generosity in having the most positive influence on me. Now, thanks to Ms. Lam, my life has turned around in a myriad of ways. An emotionally damaged boy is now a strong, young, black man preparing to graduate from the High School for Creative and Performing Arts in June 2003, and enter Morehouse College in September 2003, thanks to Ms. Lam's ongoing support. Thank you Ms. Lam.

The Lemonade Series

My Teacher Is My Mom

by Katie Bryant

I am not like most students. They all have their different teachers, classes, and classmates. I, on the other hand, have one teacher, no classmates, and a load of books on a worn desk. "Why?" you might ask. I'm home-schooled. My mother is my teacher and it's through this whole high school experience that we have become not only mother/daughter, teacher/student, but friends.

"Unsuccessful"…but thanks to my teacher, Who's also my Mom, I know it's only 2 letters away from being "successful"!

One breezy day in April I realized what an impact she had on my life. I had been waiting for about 3 weeks for my results from the Royal Academy of Dance in London about my major examinations. I had worked for that day for years and now it felt like my future was all in that letter that was a week late. Needless to say, it arrived. On the paper in bold letters was the word I had been dreading: "UNSUCCESS-FUL." I was crushed. My world was pulled apart, but in stepped my mother. Right then I didn't need a teacher, I didn't need a psychologist, nor counselor, I needed my mother. She comforted me like only she can. She helped me pick myself up and try again. She was right too; I tried again the next year and passed with flying colors. She is my inspiration. I love having my mother as my teacher.

Commit Without Hesitancy

by John Butcher

I've gone to the same school in the same small town all my life. Everything I did up to my last year in middle school was just 'ok.' It wasn't great; it wasn't horrible. I was one of those 'middle of the road' kids who just got by.

It was during my last year in middle school that I started to get friendly with some kids who were not such a good influence. I can see that now. They skipped school and went down to the river to smoke cigarettes. They didn't care about their schoolwork, never did their homework, and were experimenting with drugs and alcohol. I was beginning to get chummy with these guys when a very close friend of mine ran away from home. I won't go into why he ran away. That's his business. But in a small town, something like that really shocks everyone and, since all the community members know one another so well, we all knew how it devastated the family. It scared me to think that I could be in that same situation. What was there to stop me from making the same mistake my friend had made?

I had a teacher who taught me different things over the course of my education. It was what this teacher did when my friend ran away and I was getting caught up with a bad crowd that changed my life and put me on a successful path. She made it a point, during this particular period, to tell me the same thing over and over again— until she had me believe what she said. What did she tell me? That she was so happy to know me. She thanked me for being there; for even being born! She assured me, without any hesitancy, that things would be better. She told me, with total commitment, that I could do anything I decided to do. And she kept on and on, telling me these same things.

I'm graduating this spring. Since that year in middle school I've been able to get on the right path socially and be ambitious with my schoolwork. I went from the bottom of the reader ability group to one of the three best readers in the school. I've been band president for the last two years. I've volunteered to play my instrument for

The Lemonade Series

Christmas pageants and other community events. I've made the all-star area cast for One Act Play for two years now. Recently, I placed third in the state of Texas Cross-Examination Debate competition. I'll be attending Schreiner University in the fall, seeking a dual credit major in music and education. I'm going to be a teacher someday. Just like my mom. She has been a teacher in my school district for as long as I can remember. I'll just go ahead and tell you—that teacher who changed my life around—she was my teacher, and she's also my mom.

He Welded My Career
by David Cable

My first day of high school I began having trouble. I did not understand what was going on in any of my classes. I got scared, so I did not even try. Everything I did, I felt that I would fail; therefore, I pretended that I did not care.

The more I thought like this the more I failed and the worse I got. My freshmen year was just too much to bear. Everyone made fun of me and called me dumb and lazy. There were times I thought about ending it all. I felt like I let everyone down—even my family—which made life hard to live.

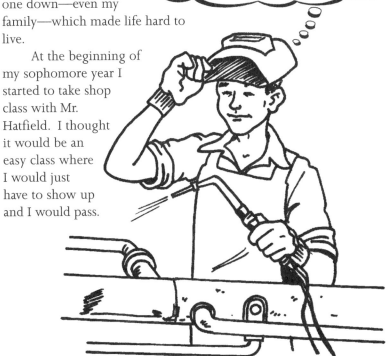

Welding! I can't wait to learn more! But, how did he know I'd love it so much?!

At the beginning of my sophomore year I started to take shop class with Mr. Hatfield. I thought it would be an easy class where I would just have to show up and I would pass.

But it was more than that. I fell behind and stayed after school with Mr. Hatfield, so he could help me get caught up. I thought of it as another detention, so I was not looking forward to it. To my surprise I showed up after class and there he was, waiting for me. I thought he was going to yell at me. But he just talked to me. He didn't even talk to me about class. We talked about what I liked to do outside of school and about life. It was almost like he wasn't my teacher, but he was a friend. I had so much fun I stayed after almost every day to hang out.

One day out of the blue he asked me about the Cass Career Center (a vocational school open to high school students). This sparked my interest. I tried to get in but my grades were too bad. But I kept trying throughout the year.

Finally, my senior year I got into the welding program at the Cass Career Center. Mr. Hatfield told me it was on my own, but I know he fought to get me in. After starting class at the Career Center, I fell in love with welding. I wanted to be the best and I even started to take pride in my work. Not too long after, I found all of my grades in school had gone up and teachers would always tell me I had a different attitude; they told me I had a glow.

So now I am a second year senior in high school with two years of training. I have so many opportunities. I have been accepted to Universal Technical Institute for the Nascar program. I even have old teachers asking me to give speeches to their freshmen students who are in the same situation as I was four years ago.

There are still things that I have to worry about, like getting money to afford college, but no matter what happens, I know that I can make it thanks to my shop teacher, Mr. Hatfield.

Mr. Breslin, A Brilliant Man

by Miranda Church

There is one teacher in my life who has changed me for the better. He is Mr. Frank Breslin, my senior English teacher. The man has the wisdom of the world in his head, heart and soul.

Throughout school, we are taught to think. But we are never taught to delve into our minds and dig out our true feelings. We are never taught to question what was seemingly set in stone, whether by history or by society. But this year Mr. Breslin has taught me to be open-minded and not to take things for granted. He likes to explain his thoughts in this way: "Read the book, at arm's length, don't hold it close to you and accept what you are told; instead, read it, think it through and make your own opinion, because in the end, that's what counts." Mr. Breslin has also told us not to take him seriously all the time because he is only playing devil's advocate to get reactions from us. He is one of those teachers who doesn't teach just to do a job and get a paycheck. He wants every one of his students to succeed in life, and he does this by making us participate in class.

Mrs. Breslin doesn't like to lecture to us; he wants us to be involved. In class, he will play a tape of a poem we read for home-work, or a play we are reading and then we will discuss what we think it means. He wants us to read into the psychological aspects of the piece. He wants to know how we feel, if it makes us angry, or if it makes us smile or laugh. He wants us to dig into the depths of our minds and souls to see what makes us tick. The reason Mr. Breslin does this is because he wants us to graduate with a solid head on our shoulders. He wants us to know what the world is about and how it works, but he also wants us to be open to different kinds of ideas. In my opinion, Mr. Breslin has opened my mind to a whole new world of ideas, and I have become a more well-rounded person because of him. So, Mr. Breslin, I thank you from the bottom of my heart for being the best teacher I have ever had.

The Lemonade Series

Eckart Chemistry
by Crystal Cleveland

Being one of the few sophomores in chemistry, I feared for my life when the bell rang for the third period. Seniors even cringed when they thought of the periodic table, so of course I trembled at the mere mention of the word "atomic." As I sat through my first few classes of chemistry, I realized that it was not going to be as terrifying as I had imagined. A teacher named Theresa Eckart made learning what was Greek to me a total breeze and fun.

She introduced us to the labs where we made ice cream to distinguish the difference between homologous and heterologuous mixtures. She worked fun into every lesson and soon we all looked forward to chemistry class. Not because it was a course we could "fly" through, but because we were learning and it was fun. Most everyday Mrs. Eckart had some crazy antic up her sleeve, which was rarely ever related to chemistry, but always a lesson in life. She taught with excitement and enthusiasm. She was the kind of teacher that offered tutoring, and was always available after class. We felt welcomed in her class and that was what was important to her. She was the teacher that worked to make education a blast, not just for the paycheck.

One day Mrs. Eckart was not there at school. All of her students, myself included, wondered where she was. Her absence was a long one and I became bored with chemistry during this period without the crime-scene investigation labs, the wacko demonstrations that somehow always left a bizarre smell afterwards, and her everyday assurance that smart people do not have all of the answers, but know how to find them.

We were all excited when Mrs. Eckart returned to school, but she was sad and distant. She explained to all of us that there had been an extreme family emergency. You see, her young brother, who she had been very close to, was cleaning his rifle when it accidentally went off and the bullet lodged in his brain, eventually killing him. She and her family were in all of our prayers, I am sure.

Nevertheless, Theresa Eckart is a survivor. Though it took some time, she was soon back and "teaching with love and laughter" once again. She selflessly put her personal tragedy behind her for the well-being of the young people around her.

I managed an A- in the course. I know without that crazy, funky, caring and supporting teacher that I would have been lucky to bring home a C- in such a difficult class. Because of her wisdom and one-of-a-kind personality, she won't soon be forgotten at Auburndale High School, which she left last year. She nearly eliminated the failure rate in chemistry. Every student she taught and person she met was touched with her spirit. Thank you, Mrs. Eckart, for being the outlet I needed to learn to love to learn again.

The Lemonade Series

She Changed My Life

by Becci Clippinger

Annabelle Fulford, the name itself is sweet to the ear. When I was in first grade, I attended Dillard Elementary School, in Winter Garden, Florida. I was like no other kid—I had a seizure disorder. This same disorder led a lot of people to shun me as a child, and still shun me today. For example, I was not allowed to stay alone with my own Grandmother, for she was afraid I would have a seizure when I was with her. But Mrs. Annabelle Fulford was different. The first day of class, she walked in and came to my desk and said, "I want you to know you will be treated no differently than any other student in my class." This was no surprise, every other teacher had said that, yet this marvelous lady was different. She never glared across the room at me. She only asked me if I felt all right when I looked like I may not, which I greatly appreciated.

Most teachers, even teachers in Middle, and High School, glared at me all day, as if at any minute I was going to fall over, have a seizure. I even had a teacher ask me every twenty-five minutes if I felt all right. Instead of making me feel secure, this attention made me feel extremely uncomfortable.

My year in Mrs. Annabelle's class was by far the best year of education for me. It was that year that I learned that even though I have a medical disorder, I was like every other kid. Since I have this medical disorder, I was very spoiled as a child, which in turn made me think that when I went to school, I didn't have to do anything but be there. To be entirely honest, I considered myself higher than other students. Mrs. Annabelle, in a rather sweet and loving way, taught me that I was not any different than any other child, which led me to believe I was also not more special than the other kids.

This was the harsh reality that taught me to become a lot less arrogant, and stubborn. She always told me that if I wanted the other kids to treat me fairly, I had to show them I was not different, and treat them in a way that I would like to be treated.

I considered Mrs. Annabelle not only a fun and entertaining

teacher, but to all of us in her class, especially me, she was a friend.

When I was younger, I never took the time to thank her for all that she taught me. By the time I realized all that she had done for me, we were hundreds of miles apart. I strongly believe the only reason I have gotten as far as I have today is because of one teacher, Mrs. Annabelle Fulford. It is from her that I got my self-esteem, and feeling of self-worth. I am sincerely grateful she was around to be my teacher.

The Lemonade Series

Importance Of Interpretation
by Camille Cohen

I remember the first day that I stepped into her classroom. I was in love immediately because there were posters all over the walls illuminated with different colors and faces, such as Billie Holiday, William Faulkner, and Langston Hughes. The seats were arranged in a square so everybody was able not only to view the teacher but each other as well. In comparison to the other dreary rooms I had encountered on my first day of high school, this last class seemed like paradise.

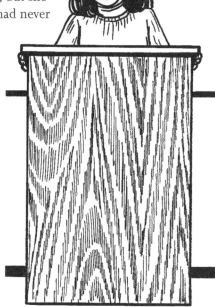

> And when she asked me to speak from my heart, everything began to change!

The teacher glided into the room. Mrs. Scott silenced the room without even opening her mouth. She wasn't mean, she wasn't drop dead gorgeous, but she carried with her a presence. I had never seen anything like it before. Her words were hypnotic. She spoke with such dignity and passion, it made me rethink the actual beauty of the English language. Mrs. Scott was confident and animated. I was clumsy and awkward. I didn't even like the sound of my own voice. She loved to have discussions on the short stories we read and she always found a way to single students out, not to embarrass them, but as I learned later, to become more familiar with the person that existed behind the name.

Initially, I hated this technique; because by doing this, she was making me go against everything I stood for, which included blending in with the other faces in the room. She would take a seemingly simple short story, mold a symbolic universal out of it, and then before actually letting us in on the greater meaning of the piece, she would choose to look me in the eye and ask my interpreted meaning. At that very moment, my mind would start to make the buzzing sound of the emergency broadcast system. Drawing a complete blank, I would look down at my desk and fumble through my words until she told me, "thank you," and moved on to somebody else's interpretation.

It went on like this for quite some time, but as the year progressed, I would find myself opening up more. When she told the class that we would be practicing public speaking, I eagerly volunteered to stand behind the podium to give my definitions of love. This was the beginning of a new life for me. For so many years I had been a private person, never letting anyone know my true feelings. My interpretation of myself lacked positive adjectives. My self-value was so low at one point that I didn't feel like waking up in the morning. I believe that Mrs. Scott spotted and analyzed this negativity. She has a gift for doing that: spotting the inner feelings of people. Her words of wisdom and honesty brought me to life and I know that I live today as a confident, independent person because of Mrs. Scott's attention and positive interpretation of me. To her I am eternally grateful. 🍃

Inspiration At A Glance

by Jessica Collier

Throughout my thirteen years of school, there has been only one outstanding teacher who has taught me, befriended me, supported me, and inspired me. Mrs. Betty Schaeffer was the one teacher in my life who helped me to become the young woman that I am today.

While looking online one day, I found the best quote that could describe what Mrs. Schaeffer has done: "The mediocre teacher tells. The good teacher explains. The superior teach demonstrates. The great teacher inspires." Upon reading this quote by William Arthur Ward, I knew that he must have been talking about Mrs. Schaeffer, the one teacher who brought inspiration to a whole new level.

I had the greatest privilege of not only having Mrs. Schaeffer for fourth grade, but for fifth grade as well. She, I believe, was, and still is, an angel in disguise.

Between kindergarten and fourth grade, I would always be found putting myself down, thinking that I was this horrible excuse for a human being, who thought that no one liked me or wanted to be my friend. I would think the worst things about myself. With this lack of self-confidence, I found it hard to trust myself, or anyone for that matter. Once I entered Mrs. Schaeffer's class, I soon found out that I was just the opposite.

Through inspiring and thoughtful conversations, Mrs. Schaeffer helped me to open up inside. I began to trust the intelligent insight that she willingly gave me. She made me realize that I am a wonder-ful, special, unique person that would make it far in life. There was never a hateful, nor hurtful comment out of her. Each and every word, sentence, or thought that issued from Mrs. Schaeffer's mouth were taken to heart, my heart. I began to see the world more openly and knew that life shouldn't be taken for granted. Mrs. Schaeffer helped me to see this with her angelic ways. For this I am forever grateful to her.

She has inspired me to become a successful young lady. With

everything that I do, I always think of my inspiration: Mrs. Schaeffer. So far, I have excelled academically, athletically, as well as philosophically. I have been in the Who's Who Among American High School Students yearbook for four years. I was nominated by the National Deans List, I am a national leader through the National Young Leaders Conference, and I was a successful runner and basketball player until I was injured. Anything and everything that I achieve in life, I will dedicate it to her. If it wasn't for Mrs. Betty Schaeffer, I wouldn't have made it this far in life with the optimistic outlook that Mrs. Schaeffer has instilled in me.

The Lemonade Series

Bring On The Sharks
by Lauren Connolly

As a sophomore in high school, I thought I had everything figured out. I had been taking voice lessons since the seventh grade, singing at various concerts for as long as I could remember, and I received the lead role in my school's musical, "How to Succeed in Business Without Really Trying." People would approach me randomly and tell me how lucky and talented I was. I believed them, perhaps too much. I knew that performing was what I wanted to do with the rest of my life and that I already had everything it took to get there.

Junior year came soon enough, and so did a reality check. I had auditioned for the Musical Theatre department at the BOCES Cultural Arts Center at the end of my sophomore year. Things were extremely different there. I wasn't surrounded with my usual praise. I was no longer a big fish in a little pond.

It was there that I met Bert Michael, an energetic man with a fiery passion for acting. He was by far the toughest teacher I have ever dealt with in my life. Each time a student would step up and perform his song or monologue for the class he would critique them. That's what he called it, "critique," but I always seemed to think the phrase, "ripping you apart," was more appropriate. He would pick apart the performance and harshly explain how it needed to be fixed. If someone didn't put enough work into their piece, he always knew and never let them get away with it. In short, he knocked us down, but I soon came to realize that it was only to build us back up again to be stronger than ever. He was offering each one of us the knowledge we needed to improve ourselves as artists, if we were willing to take it and work for it.

In a way, it seems Bert was testing us. Knocking us down to see if we would get back up again. To see how much we really wanted it. Me, I chose to embrace all that this man had to offer and get up each time I fell. Sure, I would have bruises from the fall, but ultimately, they would only make me stronger. I learned more than I could have ever imagined by taking on Bert's methods of acting and applying them to myself.

I have now learned that there are no shortcuts in life. It's not enough to want something; I've got to work for it to make it a reality. If that means I have to take a few more hits before I'm ready to face the world, then so be it. I'm ready for the challenge. I have overcome the sea full of fish, and now I am ready to take on the ocean full of sharks. All thanks to a man named Bert.

Stretch your body and expand your mind.

Dad's Lemonade Stand

Tips on Living with Love, Laughter and Lemonade!

The Lemonade Series

I Would Die For You

by Kyndra Connor

The summer before my junior year was a terrible summer. I had just moved, again, for the third time since high school started and I was feeling pretty low. I had no friends, and it was really hard to meet anyone. I tried to get a job, but kept being turned down. I felt alone, like no one cared. And if anyone did care, they didn't live within 100 miles of me. I had just turned sixteen and was looking forward to driving, but after the move, there was no chance of me getting a car anytime soon. I just felt lowly and worth nothing. It was a terrible feeling, so I tried to make myself feel better by hanging out with my sister. I did everything with her, but it made me feel worse, because I knew out there, someone was thinking, "That girl is so lame, she has to hang out with an eleven year old." I didn't like who I was, but in truth, I hadn't even given myself a chance.

School couldn't come soon enough in my book, and on the first day, I set out for school scared and excited. My stomach was aflutter with butterflies, and I couldn't wait to start making friends. My first class was my favorite! Concert band! The teacher came into the classroom right behind me. He marched right through a mess of chaos and madness, up to the board, wrote his name and said, "HELLO! I'm Mr. Washburn." The band room became still and everyone grew quiet. That was my very first impression of this teacher who very easily could be mistaken for a student. He demands respect. Quite an attribute. His first speech of the year was about Columbine. He talked about that day when he was in class at the University of Nebraska and saw the news footage. He had to make the toughest decision in his life. Would he be willing to die for his future students? He said yes. As my teacher stood at the front of the room, with his eyes brimming with tears, he talked about how he believed in us, how he wanted to inspire us to be the best. As he talked, I remember feeling moved by his unashamed ability to be so open with us. On that day he inspired me. He made me want to be a teacher.

I've become good friends with Mr. Washburn in my two years at Green River High, and he's been an awesome source of support for me. He encouraged me to challenge myself and to step up to the plate when I had to. I've also made a ton of friends in band, through music. Life couldn't be better right now for me. Mr. Washburn is just a great person. I want to have that same warm-hearted personality... that same ability to move people.... I want to make a difference, just like he made a difference in my life.

Real Music
by Bethany Corriveau

"I don't want to do it anymore," I said. "That's it." "I want you to," she said. "Give it a month." We glared at each other, neither willing to back down. Of course, since my mother had more experience (not to mention grounding power), she eventually won. That is why, on the first day of eighth grade, I trudged into school dragging a cello.

Last year, when I signed up for music, I was so excited that I couldn't sleep. Finally a real orchestra! Hah. The entire class ended up quitting, so at the end of seventh grade, the orchestra consisted of a violin and two cellos. The teacher didn't know what she was doing. I didn't care to find out if she'd be back.

> From low down to Hoedown, playing the cello has changed my life !

The first day of eighth grade should have been a blast. I, however, couldn't shake off my dread of orchestra, which was my last class. All through lunch I contemplated skipping. What would they do to me if I just left? I decided staying in orchestra was the lesser evil, even if I only had to do it for a month, and grumpily grabbed my cello. There were only seventh graders and new eighth graders in the class. I didn't know anyone. The teacher waved as I came in. "Hello! I'm Mr. Ellis. Welcome to orchestra." He walked around the room, handing out lesson books and signing out instruments. "I see you have your own cello," he said. "It's a rental. It's not really mine," I told him, thinking, yeah, a rental. It goes back in a month and I'll never play it again. "Well, it's good we have a cellist," Mr. Ellis replied. "Okay, get set up!" We started going through the lesson book. I sighed; it'd be the same as last year, just stupid exercises, because they didn't know how to teach anything else.

I counted down the days. "One week left," I told my mother, who rolled her eyes. But the next day, we found on our stands a new piece of music. "Hoedown? What's Hoedown?" Probably just another stupid exercise. "We're going to sightread today," Mr. Ellis said, winking. Wait, does that mean real music? He lifted the baton, said, "One, two, ready, play," and off we went.

Real music! To anyone else it must have been terrible. Despite the exercises we still had a lot to learn. But to me, it was the most beautiful sound in the world, everyone playing separate parts and yet, somehow, all together. Mr. Ellis didn't stop there. He gave us more music and taught us how to play and play well. I couldn't get enough. I went on to join three different civic orchestras, as well as playing in the school orchestra throughout high school. I love playing music and I can't imagine my life without it. But if it hadn't been for Mr. Ellis, I would have quit altogether and never known real music.

Thank you for that, Mr. Ellis.

The Lemonade Series

A Hero
by Claudia Dimanche

"Claudia, get your head off that desk and sit up straight. I am teaching here. This is not your bedroom, this is a class room, young lady!" my teacher Ms. Kirchner said to me once in my ninth grade year of school. Yes, she was talking to me! I was one of the young ladies who used to sleep in class, talk while the teacher was talking, do my homework in class, and copy other students. I was the young lady teachers disliked and parents thought wasn't going to accomplish anything in life.

I always thought I had no talents because I can't really sing, dance, or rap. Those three categories were what teenagers thought were talents. Everything else was stupid and a waste of time to them. Well, in Ms. Kirchner's eyes I had a talent. All I had to do was work on it and, to her, my talent would get better as days went by.

I listened to her. I practiced and practiced and practiced like a crazy child. Everyday, all I was doing was reading and writing. Sometimes, instead of going outside to chill with my friends, I read and wrote.

Giving her one of my first short stories to read, Ms. Kirschner was amazed after she read it and she got emotional. She has made a big difference in my life. Before Ms. Kirchner realized I had talent in writing, all I was doing was playing in and out of class. I did nothing during my free time. Now, all I do is write. Because of Ms. Kirchner, I now have someone to talk to even though it is a white sheet of paper. I now have a best friend.

My writing has now become a part of my life. Before, I did not know what I wanted to be after I graduate. Now, I know that I want to be a writer. I want to write screenplays, books, editorials, and short stories. Because of Ms. Kirchner's realization and her not giving up on me, I have gained a lot of knowledge. I read more than often now. I read books that are non-fiction, fiction, and books that are classics in and out of the U.S. Those books make my writing better because, I learn the writing styles of those authors and change it into a way I can use it.

My reading and pronunciation is now better because of Ms. Kirchner. I am the girl who sits up in class, pays attention, and in the first ten percent to get the work done. Lazy is not part of me anymore. Ms. Kirchner is a hero and every written work I've done is because of her. Everything I have fulfilled probably wouldn't have been fulfilled if it wasn't for her inspiration and creativity. Ms. Kirchner has changed my life. She helped me find the road I want to travel. I love her as much as I love my mom. She is a hero.

Major Hall's Chosen Few
by Katherine Dozier

Major Hall. Even his name sounds ominous, and when matched to the stories of utter terror that his old students vehemently told us, I was beyond petrified. Filled with my preconceived trepidation of him, when I first staggered into his room, I had no idea what overwhelmingly positive effects the treacheries of Mr. Hall would eventually have on me.

I still remember exactly what our first night's homework was in his class—we were assigned to discuss the theme of the poem, "The Few." Similar to "The Road Not Taken" by Robert Frost, the poem means that in order to succeed, one must choose the more difficult paths in order to receive ultimate glory in life. I turned in my paragraph response, and was shocked to receive a check minus.

I was outraged, as I had grown quite accustomed to receiving praise from my English teachers, so much that I was arrogantly expecting it again. But, no. Mr. Hall explained to me that I had not gone in depth enough, that I had not looked at every word and deciphered it—in short that my work was rather mediocre. I was obstinate in my belief that he "just didn't like me." This problem became an everyday pattern. I would work hard, and always seem to land on a B. I was always tenacious, although notably I thought I deserved an A.

Then Mr. Hall revealed that we would be reading Shakespeare's "Macbeth." When we read the first scene aloud in class, Mr. Hall asked me to be the first witch.

"Double, Double, Toil and Trouble. Cauldron burn and cauldron bubble," I said with the most mystifyingly magical cackle ever.

He asked me what those words meant, and I must have talked for 5 minutes about those two lines, because I finally understood that each word had its own distinct meaning. But that wasn't all that Mr. Hall planned to teach me. He told me to go back and read that poem from the first day of school, "The Few."

The next day in class, he asked me to define a person who is one of "The Few," and I responded by saying, "They are tenacious, determined, at times struggling, brave, stubborn people who are gifted in their abilities so much that they know that if they keep trying, then they will make it. And, in the end, 'The Few' always do make it—as a result of their own unwavering bravery."

Major Hall proceeded to coyly smile, which grew broader with each second of the pause that followed my definition. "You know," he said, "I have this student who wants to succeed in my class. She has tenaciously toiled over my homework, channeled her stubbornness into brave determination, and has confidence in her abilities. Therefore, what must this mean, Katie?"

"That she is one of The Few," I spoke slowly, catching on.

"Yes," Mr. Hall whispered. "You are."

My Teacher My Friend

by Frankie Eskridge

Entering into high school is the most electrifying moment in your life. You get to meet and know mature teenagers with adult and sometimes difficult problems. Never in my lifetime did I think I would be one of those teenagers with a difficult problem that was so hard and confusing to solve.

Partying and hanging out at all times of the night was what I was doing every weekend and sometimes on school nights. However, I always kept my GPA at 3.5 or better so no one would think anything suspicious. My friends and I met up with some boys who my friend said she knew for at least a month. They took us to the liquor store and we went past their friends' house for some mysterious reason. Then, we headed back to their house and started to drink. Not putting a limit to my drinking, I drank at least six cups of hard liquor, back to back. By that time I passed out. I woke up the next day and I was laying in a puddle of something wet. My clothing was removed from my body and was placed all around me. I went to the bathroom to urinate and forgot that I put a tampon on. When I went to reach for it, it was gone. I came to find out it was so far in my vaginal area that I had to get it removed by my personal doctor.

Attending school wasn't fun for a while because I wasn't me. Or at least that's what everyone told me. I started not to care about life, I began to think that no one loved me, and I thought that if I told my male friend that I was socializing, he would treat me differently. It got so bad that I thought my male friend was trying to sexually assault me. My favorite teacher in the whole world, Ms. Stanley, knew something was wrong. Out of nowhere, my grades started slipping and my attitude towards everyone was ambiguous. She pulled me into her office and asked me what was wrong. Instantly, I started to cry. At that point she definitely knew something was wrong with me. I broke down and told her everything. She comforted me and was there for me like no one else. She told me about her date rape situation and how it changed her life for the good. The way she broke my situation down was remarkable. She helped me get my life back on track and helped me regain a relationship with my mother.

Having a close relationship with my teacher was not something intentional. I guess it was destined from the creator above that she and I were connected. However, if I never had that talk with her I probably would have dropped out of school and maybe even have killed myself. Instead, my GPA is better than ever and I'm counseling students that have been in a similar situation.

Teaching With Love And Laughter

by Debra Evans

I look back fondly on my days at George Wolf Elementary. I remember it as a place where I was both nurtured and encouraged to grow in many ways. There is one person, though, that I definitely won't forget...

Let me take you back to the days of my not-so-distant youth, to a time where my friends and I were what defined George Wolf as a school, where teachers seemed as famous as celebrities, and where the most earth-shattering event was forgotten homework. Let me take you back to the days of my 2nd grade school year.

The first thing you'll notice is my 2nd grade teacher, Mrs. Kovacs, a warm, sweet woman who made us all feel right at home. She was the first teacher who recognized my love for writing and went out of her way to encourage me to write. It's funny that the one thing I can distinctly remember her saying is that she really loved being our teacher, but it saddened her that so many of us would forget her by the time we were in 5th grade. I just want her to know that she was wrong! I'm in 10th grade now and I STILL remember the way we would repeat the months of the year each morning... I STILL remember the journals we kept...I STILL remember the way she changed my life forever and opened me up to the world of writing.

Now let me take you back to my 6th grade graduation. What an emotional day! I was so scared to leave grade school and move to the uncertainties of junior high. After the ceremonies, my mom and I went to find Mrs. Kovacs to thank her and say farewell. I never expected what would come next...

We walked into the familiar classroom where I could remember so much comfort. I smiled as I saw Mrs. Kovacs, still looking the same way I remembered her—yet something was different. She came up to me and told me how proud she was of me—how she always knew I had a gift for writing. We started talking about our futures and what was in store for us. That's when she revealed something that has stayed with me to this day. Mrs. Kovacs told us that her cancer had come back and she didn't think she had to long to live. I couldn't believe what I was hearing; it seemed so impossible. Suddenly she was crying. "It's just that I have so much to live for." She sobbed, immediately apologizing for crying in front of us. We hugged each other and I comforted her. I was so glad that we took the time to talk to her. I then said goodbye to Mrs. Kovacs, knowing I would not see her again...

Some teachers have a way of leaving their fingerprint on the souls of their students. Mrs. Kovacs is that teacher for me. She will live within my heart forever.

The Lemonade Series

A Teachers Big Impact

by Kristen Ford

In sixth grade, my mother remarried and we moved from Orange County to San Diego. Being only 10, I found it hard to have to readjust to a new place and meet new friends. Arriving at this big new school, I was very nervous and scared, and I wanted to make a good first impression. And then my mother did the most embarrassing thing a mother could do. At lunch I was sitting at a table and when I looked up, here was my mother walking into the lunch area with all the kids. But now I understand when she says that she was only "checking on her baby." After being embarrassed, I went to my last class of the day. Ms. Horne was my teacher's name. From the beginning, I have to honestly say that I thought she was a weirdo, but I liked her

> Now, let's toast to another Thing that makes you unique!

a lot. She made learning math and science fun, which I never thought could be fun. She was always there for me to talk to, and I was never embarrassed to ask for her help. Through the next year I would always stay after school with her and help her grade papers and she would help me with my homework. I always remember her drinking her favorite soda, Diet Coke. I used to love sharing one with her. She always made me feel so good inside. She gave me the greatest sense of security. I was able to talk to her as though she was my mother. She would give me advice about friends, guys and girl things. And one of the sweetest things she did for me was, everyday, she would tell me one unique thing about me. Sometimes it would be dumb and funny, and other times, it would be a truly sincere comment. Through the next two years, our relationship became more of a friendship, and it could not have been a more perfect time to find such a great friend like her. My mother and I were going through tough times at home. My stepfather was not the greatest guy, and it was extremely hard for me to see my mother go through so much pain because of him. But because of the love my teacher gave me, I was able to continue going through school with a 4.0 GPA. I was voted a secretary of our school's ASB, and I joined the track team because Ms. Horne was going to be the coach and she really wanted me to join. Because of the positive influence my teacher had on me, I was able to make it through tough times with an optimistic attitude. By the end of 8th grade, my mother and stepfather divorced. My mother and I ended up moving closer to where Ms. Horne lived. And since I have been attending high school, we have kept in touch and seen one another on a regular basis. She is my positive angel. Thank you, Ms. Horne.

The Most Important Lesson
by Blake French

Over the years, many people enter and leave our lives, events occur and are forgotten, and many sorts of circumstances will be overcome. Regardless of how dramatic or insignificant, however, I believe all things happen for a reason. Sometimes, we are not aware of the reason until a drastic change occurs; other times, the reason presents itself instantly. As I learned a few years back, my experience with one person alone completely changed the direction of my future, and the journey began with the most unlikely of circumstances.

Throughout much of middle and high school, I hid myself inside a personal security bubble. As an awkward, naïve adolescent, I entered junior high without many friends but carried with me numerous individualistic peculiarities. Therefore, I immediately became a prime target of unspeakable ridicule from other students. As my foes accumulated, my self-confidence diminished. I began to alienate myself from everyone around me, including my supportive family members. I drew a profoundly negative outlook on the world and people in my life, as I graduated into high school. Eventually, these painful emotions spiraled out of control, and I began to rebel against school officials, family members, and even my limited number of friends.

Then I reached sophomore year in high school and everything began to change. A rather unique English teacher challenged me on a deeper lever than other teachers had in the past. I felt that this individual actually did care about my future. As he unraveled emotions and sparked my attention, I initially made enemies with him, attacking his imperfections and even speaking to the principal about our substantial disagreements. Though, through all my bickering and complaining, he continued to recognize my talents and treat me like a real person. I soon realized this was no ordinary English teacher, but a wonderful, caring person unlike any teacher I had ever met before.

As the months continued, the teacher supported me emotionally and academically, and still does to this day. He's been a tremendous influence in my life over the past several years, and I will never forget the impact he has made on my future. If not for my experience with this teacher, I don't believe that I would have invested enough time and effort into my future or believe in myself enough to apply to Pepperdine University at this time. He helped me gain the confidence to change from an uncomfortable, belittled teenager into a confident, proficient young man. All because he bothered to care.

The Lemonade Series

Important Lessons In Life And Music

by Lauren Gage

The most influential teacher I have ever known was my former viola teacher, Martin Fischer. He taught me so much about music and life, lessons that I will never forget. When I met Mr. Fischer, he was a retired professor and I was just switching from violin to viola. He immediately started me on a strict regiment of exercises and etudes, trying to build up my basic technique. I longed for a real piece, but he refused to let me go on until he thought I was truly ready. I didn't understand it, but I now see the way he prepared me for the kind of repertoire that I am performing now, even after just five years. Music was not the only thing that I learned from him; I learned patience, persistence, and how rewarding music can be.

Mr. Fischer had an interesting past. He graduated from Julliard, although he had to leave to serve in the Second World War. He studied with one of the most prominent violists in the world at the time, Milton Katims. He used to tell me about the fun that he had at Julliard, which was where he met his wife, a soprano, and made the most of his professional connections. There were pictures on his wall of famous musicians, including Isaac Stern and Mstislav Rostropovich, playing with the university orchestra while Mr. Fischer conducted. His connections and stories not only interested me but also inspired me. I came to realize that I wanted a life like his: full and rewarding.

I still cannot believe how patient he was with me, and I understand now how truly awful my playing was, sometimes. He carefully worked with me to develop my ear and shape my hand properly. He would stop me in the middle of a phrase or line and tell me that I was flat. Then I would move my finger ever so slightly—and at first I couldn't even tell the difference—and he would say that the pitch was there, not where I had been before. I gradually started to hear the tiniest differences in pitch, and my playing improved dramatically. I honestly believe that I would not be attending a conservatory next year had I not studied with Mr. Fischer, even though I was only with him for a few years. He would come to my house, sometimes, or ask to see me again in the middle of the week. He never charged for these extra lessons; he was only eager to teach me because he knew I was eager to learn. I only hope that I can be as talented and influential a teacher as he was to me when I begin to give lessons after I graduate from college. He taught me about the beauty in music and the beauty in life.

Believe in yourself and focus on your goals.

Dad's Lemonade Stand

Tips on Living with Love, Laughter and Lemonade!

Connecting Beneath The Skin

by Caroline Glagola

Union Springs, Alabama is no more than an intersection of highways. It is not even important enough to be listed on a map key. It is one of the many small southern towns now seeing its beautiful houses crumble, its prom queens gracefully age, and its champion field trial dogs begin their peaceful sleep in the local hound dog cemetery. Union Springs' quiet oak-lined streets and fields of wildflowers, however, hold a different meaning for me. The hidden charms of small town life in the deep south hide the truths of injustice and abuse that human nature harbors.

Genealogy can uncover strange things, and sometimes family trees have roots that run deeper than one can imagine. My family tree includes Patricia Phillips, my ninth grade African-American English teacher, the descendant of slaves from the small town of Union Springs, and a member of my Caucasian family. She changed the way that I look at my past.

Although I did no injustice to this woman, this virtual stranger, my kin, I felt a sense of indebtedness, that somehow I owed her recompense. I believed that I could not apologize enough. My shame over the sins of my forefathers—their merciless treatment of slaves, HER forefathers—was not only my past, but my albatross. Patricia Phillips, however, refused my attempts at reconciliation insisting that no wrong had befallen her. She taught me many things that year: grammar, punctuation, tone, and diction, but, more importantly, she taught me that the past is not something to shame, but to remember. She personalized a history that I would never have so deeply understood, and I learned that family is not determined by skin color, but by a connection, one that we will share forever.

He Saved My Life
by Megan Goracke

My seventh grade science teacher not only changed my life, he saved it. His name was Mr. Lillquist, and it was his first year teaching. I was a great student. I had straight A's, and was very involved. No one would have ever guessed anything was wrong with me. But there was something wrong, I was severely depressed. I didn't let on to anyone that anything was wrong with me. I kept everything inside me. The only thing that made me feel better was cutting myself. That's right; I was a "cutter."

Finally, the time came when I couldn't keep it to myself anymore. I exploded. I confided to three of my best friends. They were seventh graders and didn't know what to do or say. I begged them not to tell anyone else, so they were just as scared and confused as I was. Eventually they convinced to me to go talk to a teacher. I decided Mr. Lillquist was the teacher I wanted to talk to, so two of my best friends and I went to talk to him.

Mr. Lillquist was terrified. He had no idea what to do! He had no idea what to say! But I will never forget his empathy and support. He told me I would be okay. He told me of all my strengths. But the best thing he did for me was to make me tell my parents what I was doing. Without the strength of Mr. Lillquist, I don't think I would have ever told my parents. My sickness would have gotten much worse.

My parents got me help. I was in treatment for months. Now, five years later, I am much better. My depression may never be completely gone, but I will never get so bad again that I would ever hurt myself. I thank every day of my life that I had Mr. Lillquist as a teacher. He saved my life.

The Lemonade Series

A Teacher & Friend

by James Greco

I've always been told that teenage years are the toughest. Mine started out that way until I met a special teacher named Anthony Riley.

When I was just 3 months old, I was taken away from my parents, and placed in foster care until my grandparents were awarded custody. The responsibility of raising me was not an easy task due to my anger and violent temper. In time, my grandmother became ill, and my grandparents were unable to raise me. At the age of 11, I was placed back into foster care, where I lived in 4 homes, each one becoming more and more abusive. I received news one morning that my grandmother had passed away. I wanted to be by her side, but I could not go to her funeral because I was on my way to a group home, where my life would be changed forever.

All I want is a Foster Father—But will you do it?

In an instant I lost everything. I felt a huge void in my life and fear of the unknown. I needed stability. My performance in school was poor and I resented almost everyone. One morning I received a call from the director of the group home, asking me if I wanted to attend a charter school where his friend was principal and teacher. I didn't care at the time, so I said, "Yes."

I met Anthony the following week when I went to enroll in the school. It was awkward at first, but Anthony tried to make me feel comfortable. As a part-time teacher, he allowed me a sense of normalcy, and in different ways we connected. After a few months in the group home, I realized I was becoming more depressed. I was looking at a newspaper one day, and saw an advertisement for foster parents. I cut out the ad and gave it to Anthony. He was puzzled and asked, "What is this?" I then said, "I want you to become my foster parent." He was a little taken aback, but said that he would give it some thought.

Later on in the evening he called, and began to tell me about his life, that he was single, no children, worked in television production, which might take him out of town frequently, and he would have to make tremendous adjustments to his lifestyle. My heart sank as I heard him take a deep breath and say, "But I will do it anyway." Those words were one of the greatest gifts in my life. On October 25, 2001, Anthony became my foster parent and in January 2003, he became my legal guardian.

Anthony has given me love and a feeling of safety. My academics have improved. I am graduating as a honor student and pursuing my dreams of going to tech school. What is so unique is that I've learned the importance of watching over one another, and helping each other down the road of life. Anthony has taught me, when life gives you lemons, you make lemonade.

He Never Gave Up

by Aaron Grove

Some students have teachers who inspire them to great heights and to pursue paths never once thought possible. My story has a little different twist. When I was a baby, I had numerous ear infections and continued to have fluid in my ears, which gave me a ringing in my ears. I had it checked by many doctors, only to be told that I would have to live with it. I found out that it affected my ability to match pitch. This wouldn't be such a great problem, except that I was born into a musical family with my dad being a music teacher. We attended many musical events, concerts, performed musical specials, belonged to the church choirs, and sang in school musicals. Daily, our lives were filled with music.

I'm sure that many thought that this was most unfortunate for my parents to have a child who couldn't match pitch. At first it might have been cute, after awhile it could possibly be an embarrassment, but they never for a second seemed to show it. My dad did some research on teaching tone-deaf children to sing. He kept insisting that I be involved in music: piano lessons, instruments, choirs, and voice lessons. He never wrote me off. I tried my best to do all these things, usually with some enjoyment of the music. During adolescence, I remember working with my dad trying to match pitch. I still was told I needed to raise or lower my pitch. He kept his encouragement and persistence. He felt it was possible to teach a tone-deaf person to sing in tune.

Well, here I am a senior in high school Only time would tell the success of all my parent's persistence. I had a high school choir teacher who got a hold of me my freshman year and was highly inspirational. Although I dropped my instruments, I was inspired to keep singing. I kept the voice lessons and was told that I was making progress. I'm sure she could have rejected me as a student when seeing what kind of project I would be, but for some reason, she didn't. She praised, inspired, and taught me correct vocal techniques. My choir director also drilled these basic techniques into our choir.

Our choirs won two Grammy Awards, got first place at contests, and won Grand Champions at show choir competitions. Much to my amazement, I made these choirs and was pushed beyond what anyone, including myself, thought possible. When my friends and I got together, we played piano and guitars and sang. I took a step of gigantic faith and performed a special act solo during my senior year. I dedicated it to my mother who was there with my father, always encouraging me. I would have to say I owe my success of breaking through the sound barrier (tone deafness) to my persistent choir teacher. My dad, who else?

The Lemonade Series

My Second Grade Teacher

by Ashley Harter

One morning, I woke up to screaming and yelling. The next thing I knew, my dad's fist was bleeding and my mom had locked herself in the bathroom. It was only 7:30 in the morning, and I had to get ready for school. My little sister, in kindergarten at the time, was crying hysterically because she didn't know what was going on. I rolled myself out of my bed, got my sister and I ready for school and left. We lived only two blocks away from school so we walked there.

I sat down at my desk like nothing ever happened. I was fine all day until we were given an assignment after lunch. My second grade teacher, Mrs. Stall, asked us to draw a picture of our family. All of my classmates started to draw their families. I put my head down on my desk and started to cry. Mrs. Stall came over to my desk and squatted down. "What is wrong, Ashley," she said, trying to comfort me.

"I don't have a family; my mommy and daddy are getting a divorce." At that point I was extremely embarrassed to be crying in front of the class. Mrs. Stall took me in the hallway and continued to talk to me. Mrs. Stall gave me a hug and said, "Don't worry, everything will be ok. My parents were divorced, and you know what?"

I looked up, tears rolling down my cheeks, and said, "What, Mrs. Stall?"

"Everything gets better. You know all the fighting? Well, it stops!"

We stood in the hallway for a few more minutes, until I calmed myself down. I went back in the classroom, afraid everyone would make fun of me, but no one did.

Mrs. Stall never knew how much that meant to me. In that moment in time, I needed someone there to tell me that everything was going to be ok. I needed an adult figure to take two seconds away from fighting and show me that they cared. I will never forget what Mrs. Stall did for me. She helped me through one of the worst times in my life. Thank you.

My Teacher, My Friend
by Megan Havens

My second grade teacher inspired me to want to become an educator. She is an example of the teacher I one day hope to be. In third grade, I began helping her classroom and tutoring her students after school. I have always enjoyed my time with her students and continue to enjoy helping. Her students and I are extremely lucky to have a teacher who cares about our future.

Even in second grade, I realized what a unique person she was. She always encouraged us and gave us challenges that were both rewarding and fun. She did a variety of activities that included the whole family. She is loved and admired by all of her students.

I once again became her student when chemotherapy and surgery kept me from being able to attend school in seventh grade. She volunteered her services to keep me up with my classes and was always available when I felt well enough to do school work. Even though the schedule was erratic, she always came to my house with a smile on her face. She always knew, without anyone saying, when I felt well enough to work or when not to give me a lot of work. Had it not been for her, I am sure I would have been struggling when I returned to school the next year.

She has become a true friend and I value the relationship and camaraderie that we share. It is rare to find someone who loves his or her job as much as she does.

She is always the first to volunteer for extra assignments. She always has a positive attitude when I show up at her classroom and I have never asked her for a favor that has been refused. I have had many good teachers throughout my school career, but have never found anyone who quite measures up to her standards.

I am currently president of the Future Educators of America, which I became a member of in high school. As future educators, we are allowed to shadow a teacher; this has given me the opportunity to observe in her classroom for full days. She is an extremely creative teacher, who always inspires her students to do their best. I hope to one day be able to use all the valuable insights I have learned from her. I look forward to being able to do my student teaching with her, or someone like her. You could not ask for a better example to follow.

I feel extremely fortunate to have her as a role model. She has a great love for her job and deeply cares about her students and our community. I hope to be able to continue the high standards she exemplifies as an educator and a person.

Look at your feet and be grateful you have shoes.

Dad's Lemonade Stand

Tips on Living with
Love, Laughter
and Lemonade!

The True Meaning Of Teaching
by Rachel Henrich

Anatole France once said, "The whole art of teaching is only the art of awakening the natural curiosity of young minds for the purpose of satisfying it afterwards." This is the way my English teacher, Ms. Nelson, touched my heart as well as the hearts of other students. She takes her job to another level and reaches out to students. She helped me explore my abilities in writing and in the process helped me explore who I am as a person

In my English 10 class, Ms. Nelson assigned a portfolio project; we had to pick a specific topic and write various essays about that topic. She told us to pick a topic that meant something to us because it would be easier to write when you have a feeling about the topic. The previous summer my brother, Eddie, committed suicide and that was an event in my life that held great importance. However, I decided that writing about suicide would be too depressing at that point in my life. Ms. Nelson and I talked about different possibilities and we agreed that it would be best for me to do a tribute to both my brothers by simply making my topic, "Brothers." Throughout the project, I struggled putting my ideas and feeling into words. Ms. Nelson was always there to help me develop my ideas and always listened to what I had to say. She was very encouraging when it came to my work and helped make me become a more confident writer. She was very supportive of me and my writing through out the whole project.

During the two months that I was writing about my brothers I had trouble expressing how I felt, especially when it came to Eddie and his death. Ms. Nelson was always very understanding and considerate about my feelings. She listened to anything I needed to talk about, whether it was pertinent to my essay or not. I was able to confide in her about my brother and how I was feeling, even feelings that I was not comfortable telling other people. She was always very reassuring and made me realize that I would become a stronger person because of my loss.

The Lemonade Series

Again, repeating what Anatole France once said, "The whole art of teaching is only the art of awakening the natural curiosity of young minds for the purpose of satisfying it afterwards." Ms. Nelson helped me grow as a person as well as a writer. She gave me hope when I felt I had none. Most teachers do not go out of their way to help students the way that she helped me. She awakened the curiosity inside of me not only about my writing, but also about myself. Thank you, Ms. Nelson!

Last Names And Simple Abundances
by Kelli Hogan

The first day of my senior year of high school, I stood in front of my Spanish class, clutching my schedule in a nervous fashion. The sheet of paper read: "Spanish IV—Miriam Grimmer". Truthfully, looking at that name brought me fear. I did not know Mrs. Grimmer, but to me, her name sounded like the grim reaper and connoted uneasiness and anxiety. When the bell rang, I slowly stepped inside the classroom.

She was from Cuba—dark skinned, black hair, and lips as red as roses. I remember thinking that she was one of the most beautiful women I had ever seen. She looked at me and smiled. I smiled back and immediately, all of my fears diminished. Who knows? Maybe she wasn't like the grim reaper after all.

The next couple of months after that, my grandma became seriously ill. She had been diagnosed with ovarian cancer and we were just starting to see the effects of her chemotherapy treatment. She was constantly in the hospital, which meant my mom and dad were no longer home as much as usual. It was up to my two sisters and I to take care of the house and to make sure our six-year-old brother was doing his homework. If anyone has ever had to go through the emotional pain of having a sick relative, you know that it's not easy. I felt like there was nothing I could do but stand back and watch my grandma slip away. I couldn't stop the cancer from spreading and I certainly couldn't delay her death. I became guilty and disgusted with myself because I was completely helpless. These emotions wore me out but I did not want to talk to anyone about this because I did not want to seem selfish.

One day after Spanish class, I mentioned my grandma's hospital-ization to Mrs. Grimmer. She was very sympathetic towards me, giving me reassurance and hope. More and more, I began to open up to her and every conversation we had allowed me to get rid of some of the guilt I carried. Mrs. Grimmer surprised me one afternoon by giving me a simple abundance journal of gratitude. The purpose of this journal was to make an entry everyday of something good that you encountered. I promised Mrs. Grimmer that no matter how bad a day seemed, I would find something positive to write about. Although my grandma's conditioned worsened, the journal filled up quickly and it helped me appreciate the things I had instead of wishing for things I didn't have.

In December, when my grandma passed away, Mrs. Grimmer was there to support and comfort me. She has always been there when I need to talk, or sometimes when I just need a hug. Mrs. Grimmer has taught me three very valuable lessons: life's simple abundances must not be overlooked, teachers are the most admirable human beings, and last names do not reveal a person's character.

Write Now
by Victoria Hughes

Everyone has a gift. Unfortunately, most people's gifts go unnoticed, even by the bearer. Imagine if, after finding your gift, you are faced with one of the greatest impediments ever put before mankind—an extreme fear of rejection and humiliation. Even worse, imagine it stopped you from pursuing your gift.

For as long as I can remember, my family and close friends pushed me to write. I've had an overwhelming number of supporters compared to critics, but their voices rang hollow for me. I've always been at odds with my most cruel and outspoken critic: myself. I can honestly say I had almost no faith in my own abilities. Any time I wrote I would sit back and wonder how I could have written something so deplorable. At times, I would actually become sick to my stomach or get headaches when I thought about reading anything I wrote in front of my audience.

Then a light was relit. I was volunteering

If she believes in me, then somehow, I know...this really is my gift!

The Lemonade Series

at my old elementary school for my fourth grade teacher, Mrs. Acerra, a friend of the family and a mentor to me. She has always been a voice of praise and I respect her opinion as I do few others. While in her room I mentioned a storyline that had been bludgeoning its way around my mind. Her eyes lit up and she said to me very calmly, but in a tone not to be argued with, "You should write this down, you should be writing everything down."

Despite all the times she had voiced such opinions in the past, I began tapping at my keyboard again, yet still without real enthusiasm or hope—it was only to please her and myself to some degree. My old fears still plagued me, but her constant support motivated me to press on. One day, she suggested that I write an article for the magazine she edited. I was taken aback, I had never hoped to have anything published—that only happened to people with talent. I wrote an essay and was horribly dissatisfied, as I was with everything I put pen to.

Somehow, it made it into the magazine. Weeks later, when I saw my name inside—to be read by the largest body any of my works have encountered—something changed. It was dramatic, I saw my abilities anew. People were reading what I had to say, and enjoying it. I felt as though an entire world had been opened to me, despite the fact if you are not a Florida science teacher you will never encounter my piece. It sparked a new desire in me. I wanted people to hear my voice through my writing.

Thanks to Mrs. Acerra and her unwavering faith in me, I have found faith in myself—and I refuse to let anyone crush it. We all have gifts, but I can no longer imagine not using mine. I have broken out of my self-made bonds. I write now, and I don't intend to stop.

The Who, What And Where Of My "Special" Education

by Michael Hurt

I t all started when I went to pre-school. Unlike most so-called "normal" children my age, I was deemed to be "different" and placed in a certain group because of "problems" I was born with. This didn't allow me to interact with my peers the way "the system" wanted me to. This certain "problem" was later categorized as high-functioning autism. I entered a special pre-school for kids with physical and learning disabilities who needed special care, which was outside the local school district. Even when I was placed in a "normal" school in our school district for kindergarten and first grade, I was still put in a special education group (for multiple handicaps) separate from most of the other kids.

Due to my first grade teacher recognizing that I could handle a less restrictive environment than the one provided to me, I was sent to the school closest to my home for second grade. It was here that I met the teacher that I am writing about, Mrs. Heather O'Connell, a dedicated special education professional who was determined to help children progress through school to the best of their abilities. She is the type of person who never hesitates to reach out to help others. After having me in her class for a matter of months, she saw my potential (through my reading and math skills) not to need the level of special education that I was in. She sent me to the "regular" second grade class under the teaching skills of Miss Kelly (who fortunately had also been a special education teacher and knew how to handle "kids like me").

My advancements in second grade allowed Mrs. O'Connell to recommend me for my third grade year to the next less restrictive level of special education, the Resource room. Although she wasn't my teacher anymore, this didn't mean that she stopped helping me. She became a friend to my family and helped me to learn how to control my frustrations so they wouldn't always come out as physical rage. She even introduced my family to a local church which we still

73

attend ten years later. The church has helped us in numerous ways, one example being the youth group that my sister and I attended. This helped me to improve my social interaction with other children my age. Mrs. O'Connell was even there to act as our sponsor when my sister and I were baptized at the church. Recently, she wrote a letter of recommendation for me which I am using for college and scholarship applications. She still remains one of my family's closest friends. It was due to her that I was able to progress through school without the need of constant special aid, and have now reached the least restrictive level which is a consultant teacher. I will always be grateful for all the help and encouragement that Mrs. O'Connell has given me.

The Lasting Ripple

by Kelly Iwanabe

As one of one hundred and forty-six students, it is quite easy to get lost in the numbers. Seeing each student for only an hour a day gives minimal time to truly connect with each gregarious teenager. Many teachers will explain and elaborate on lessons if extra help is necessary, but few will invest time in their students' personal lives. Until recently, I firmly believed that work and business should always be kept separate from personal family life. The actions of one individual, my teacher, will forever change my impression of kindness.

During a school trip, a roommate confided in her horrifying experiences of abuse at home. Never before had she told a soul. Sensing her desperation and plea for help, I felt lost, fearing who to turn to for guidance. Filled with despair, all I knew was she needed immediate support and love. Fortunately, fate has a way of unfolding its mysteries. Upon returning to school, I quickly turned to the only person who I knew would have the answers, Mrs. Scrivner, my AP English teacher. Always making sacrifices for her students, Mrs. Scrivner had my confidence that all would be resolved. Mrs. Scrivner is not only a teacher, but also an approachable mentor and friend to all of her students. She immediately advised me to encourage my roommate to seek her help, as a trustworthy friend. With Mrs. Scrivner's reassurance, my roommate instantly had a strong foundation of love and guidance. Never leaving her side, Mrs. Scrivner awaited the social worker and police reports. Although my roommate's mother and father brutally beat her, she finally understood what love truly was, as a result of Mrs. Scrivner's support.

Even though she is still living in a group home and waiting to be adopted, my roommate's outlook and attitude about life has positively changed as a result of Mrs. Scrivner's constant reassurance. Seeing the hope and energy in the eyes of my roommate makes me appreciate my role model, Mr. Scrivner. She rescued my roommate with hope and kindness. Mrs. Scrivner is not only a teacher who has enlightened

The Lemonade Series

me about "Julius Caesar" and "Grapes of Wrath," but also has taught me about the beauty of helping others. Regardless of the circumstances, Mrs. Scrivner never lost faith in my roommate. Knowing that she would do the same for each of her students teaches me about unconditional love and support. Mrs. Scrivner has inspired me to reach out and make a positive impact on the world. Encouraging me to become active in helping abused teenagers, Mrs. Scrivner has guided me with support. I am currently involved at a local children's shelter, comforting teenagers who, like my roommate, are in a state of hopelessness. Following Mrs. Scrivner's example, I hope to touch people's lives as she does. Her love for her students has shown me the truth behind the statement, "It is not what I gain, but what I give that measures the life I live."

Friendship Through Music
by Danielle Jefferis

I magine, for a minute, how many people you come in contact with on a daily basis. How many would you say? Ten to twenty? Maybe even forty to fifty? When I think back to how many people I've been in contact with throughout my life the number seems astronomical. Trying to remember them all would be next to impossible. But there is one incredible person that rises above all the others. This person has made an enormous impact on my life and he will remain in my heart and mind forever.

He accepted nothing but greatness from his orchestra... But could I pay the price?

Mr. Carlos Elias is an extremely talented violinist and conductor from El Salvador who has traveled across the world showcasing his gift. Just five years ago he relocated to become the head of the string department at Mesa State College. I, who had just recently moved as well, began studying with him through private violin lessons. While at first he did intimidate with his immeasurable musical ability and thick Latin accent, it didn't take long to get to know him. I began to look forward to my biweekly lessons. Later, I auditioned for Carlos and was chosen to join his Mesa State Symphony Orchestra. This was such a big honor for me because I was one of his youngest members. I greatly anticipated each concert and loved having the opportunity to perform professional pieces at Carlos' extremely high levels of performance and expectations. And those levels are some of the things that I admire most about this man. Through stories of his childhood, growing up in El Salvador, I have seen how thankful he is for being a musician, for being an American, and for having the opportunity to share his talent with students like me. He accepts nothing from his orchestra but greatness because he knows that we can achieve it. Just when we may feel like giving up, Carlos pushes us one step further. He is what teachers are meant to be. And not only that, Carlos Elias is what friends are meant to be. No matter what problem I may be experiencing, his priority is to talk through it and help fix it. Recently, I came to him ready to quit his orchestra because I could not afford to pay the tuition this semester. I was extremely upset and, although he understood, he wouldn't let me quit. He explained to me how much he wanted me in his orchestra and how saddened he would be to see me give up music. He then gave me a $300 scholarship, enough to cover my tuition, allowing me to continue music. That small act of kindness alone overwhelmed me enough to bring me to tears. Through his deep kindness and compassion, I have developed an incredible teacher-student relationship and, even more importantly, a wonderful friendship. Carlos Elias is an amazing musician, teacher, and friend. He has taught me responsibility, discipline, honor, and humility, and I will forever be grateful for his involvement in my life.

In The Making
by Jamie Jetton

"With a loud yell, I threw open the lantern and leaped into the room…"

I felt shivers go down my spine and leaned forward at my desk; so engrossed in the narration, I didn't bother to mask my eagerness. His words were read so eloquently and with so much animation that I was instantly drawn into the excitement of Poe's, "The Tell-Tale Heart."

He jumped from behind the podium and slammed his hand on my desk, causing me to reel back in start. My heartbeat thudded rapidly against my ribs and I gripped at my jeans in an effort to calm myself down. With flaming cheeks, I heard a few snickers from the back of the room, causing me to slide farther down my seat in embarrassment. Sometimes I hated getting so caught up in Mr. Pullen's stories. Slinking into a conspirator-like huddle, he smiled and continued, fully

My heartbeat thudded rapidly against my ribs, and I gripped my jeans in an effort to calm myself down!

immersed in the character and projecting that same passion to the rest of the class. When he finally snapped his old book shut, I sat up and blinked, only then realizing that I had been blocking the rest of the classroom out and merely focusing on his words.

"And that...is Poe. Comments? Critiques? Signs of life?" Mr. Pullen asked casually as he returned to his throne behind the podium.

Hands immediately went up and the classroom was thrown into discussion. I looked around in amazement, hardly believing that my peers would show such eagerness to participate now when they hadn't in the previous years.

I sat back and studied him while he listened intently to what everyone had to say. You never really see your teachers as real people. They just magically appear to make you work and stress the importance of an education. Then I noticed something about Mr. Pullen that I never had before. He wore this look while everyone was commenting on what he read, as if he were trying not to show how happy and proud he was. Ocassionally, though, his eyes would sparkle and he'd beam if a student knew what Poe was trying to convey. It was afterwards that I really looked around. There was this enthusiasm in everyone, like they were affected as much as me by his reading. I wanted to be able to move people that much. I wanted to stand in front of a class and get the same look he had received.

At the end of the year, Mr. Pullen pulled me aside and handed me a wrapped package before simply smiling and walking away. I raced home, barely containing my excitement as my fingers tore impatiently at the paper. Hardly believing what I saw, I shakily opened the book cover, reading the written words carefully through my tears. 'Here's to your future. May you draw from it the inspiration that I did.'

"And that...is Poe," I see myself saying, snapping shut the tattered book given to me years earlier and turning back to my class. "Comments?"

Learn How You Are Not Stupid, But If You Keep It Up, You Will Be

by Corie Kellman

Growing up, children are always told, "No question is a stupid question." I never quite understood that. For the majority of my school years, I felt like many of my fellow classmates who were too embarrassed to ask a question for fear of sounding dumb. Going into my junior year of high school, you'd think a straight-A student, like me, would be comfortable with challenging their knowledge. Hah! That's a joke if I have ever heard one. I was terrified of asking questions. The way I viewed it was, "If I don't understand, it's no big deal; no one else around me understands either." Oh, but what a vicious cycle that is. Being bright, I should have realized, "If I don't understand, ask! No one else around me understands either, so I won't look stupid, because they don't know either!" Nevertheless, I was ignorant enough not to speak up and to continue listening to the words that soon mutated into muddy tones that went through one ear and out the other. However, that all changed when I took a US History class with Mr. Winter. History happened to be my least favorite subject up until I took Mr. Winter's class.

What do you really need history for, anyway? Well, I think I learned more about social skills in that class than about anything else! He should have called the course: "Learn how you are not stupid, but if you keep it up, you will be." But I'm pretty sure the school board wouldn't be able to justify it as fulfilling the Michigan high schools' requirement for US History.

Mr. Winter held onto a class list in the front of the room and marked participation points for each of his students. He required all of us to ask and answer questions, unless, of course, we wanted to retake the class next year and ask and answer questions then. It sounds like a harsh thing to ask high school students to pay attention and expand their thinking, but Mr. Winter was always nice about it. He never treated any question as stupid. In fact, the course could have also been easily named: "Ask obvious questions, raise your grade." It was often very humorous at the end of the semester when everyone would ask the simplest question in order to get points to cushion their marking period grade. He would even give participation points for irrelevant questions, even for one like, "Do you make up answers when you don't know them to make us believe you do?" He did seem to always know the answer to every question, too, which was what prompted that particular question. Mr. Winter taught me something I would have never expected to get from anyone. He taught me how to ask questions without feeling so insecure. Though Mr. Winter is no longer a teacher, he will forever be a part of my life, because he taught me one thing that is critical in learning: If you don't know, ask.

How One Teacher Influenced My Life
by Aimee Kidd

Growing up in a household where using signed English is the dominant language, I found it was hard for me to grasp the difference between the nuances of it in relation to spoken English. By the time I entered second-grade, I was behind in reading and had trouble using sign language at home and conversational English at school.

Out of exasperation, my first-grade teacher had told my parents to have me stop using sign language at home. This unfair request humiliated my father, who is profoundly deaf. Although my mother has been hard-of-hearing since childhood, she learned sign language while in high school. She speaks well enough for others to understand her. Even so, phonetics bothers her. My parents did not believe signing itself was the root of my difficulties. My second-grade teacher, Mrs. See, told my parents in an early report that I needed help in reading. My parents wanted a solution badly enough to send a note to the principal.

Soon a conference with Mrs. See, the principal and my parents was set up. After careful listening and analysis, Mrs. See determined it was not sign language but my inability to hear the phonetics at home that was most likely the fundamental problem. My parents were surprised that she was supportive of my using sign language to communicate with them, and she made an impact that has since influenced who I am today. That impact will be with me the rest of my life, for she helped me overcome my reading difficulties with phonetic tutelage every day after school. That sacrifice on her part is rare among teachers, and my ability and self-confidence in reading started rising to grade-level. I began to distinguish the difference between sign language and English usage. Fortunately, I never stopped communicating with my parents—in sign language to my father and by voice to my mother, eventually using both modes interchangeably whenever I needed to communicate with one or both.

The Lemonade Series

I found Mrs. See to be a caring person, a great mentor, a strong leader, and an excellent example of a successful teacher. Now as I graduate from high school, I realize that I could not have made it this far if it were not for her commitment, support and understanding. I am currently taking classes at a community college, as well as finishing my high school career. Education has helped me improve my communication skills, as well as critical thinking, problem solving, decision-making and social interaction skills. Without Mrs. See (and my supportive parents), I would not have found my raison d'etre in this world. Because of Mrs. See, I have decided to pursue a dream of becoming a college professor. I hope I can live up to what she instilled in me and that I will be able to encourage my future students to be the best they can be and help them pursue their own dreams.

What It Means To Be A Teacher

by Kathryn Kleohn

I entered class with a letter in my hand, and placed it on my teacher's desk before taking my seat. The night before, I'd been appalled by the lesson he had assigned us. We were asked to read Shirley Jackson's, "The Lottery," and answer five simple plot questions which I found ridiculous considering the story. As I read, I was overcome with disturbed feelings from the picture of society expressed in the text. I knew I couldn't do the assignment without protest; instead, I'd composed the letter now sitting on my teacher's desk. I explained to him that I found his assignment tasteless and inappropriate for the severity of the subject. When he finished reading the letter, my teacher quietly asked me to approach his desk. I stood, ready to defend myself. He handed me the letter, smiling, saying, "Thank you for the letter. I'm glad you learned something, but that wasn't the assignment." I sat back down in my seat, confused, but ready to learn.

When the bell rang, he had successfully coached the

What do you mean, Thank you? Aren't you going to yell at me?

class through an investigation of the ideas and messages in Jackson's story, including society's need to relieve responsibility and guilt. My teacher had challenged us to learn and explore literature. As I gathered my things, he asked if I was satisfied with the lesson. "Thank you for the lesson, the challenge, and introducing me to literature," I thought. "Yes," was all I said.

From that day on, I began to look at life and literature differently. My teacher was wonderful, involving his students in every aspect of his class. He used Styrofoam "fun noodles" to awaken daydreaming students, or as props for Shakespeare's Romeo and Juliet. He was always running around the classroom, jumping onto his chair to illustrate an important point, or pulling students from their desks when he wanted them to participate. My teacher would create poems instantly, then ask us to do the same. He dared students to learn, provoked them to prove him wrong, and challenged them to become better people. He taught me the power of teaching. By mid-year, I knew what I wanted to do with my life; I wanted to teach English and become as amazing a teacher as he. He was the first teacher who made me recognize my ambition and encouraged me to love English! He not only influenced me, he inspired me.

I've learned from over forty teachers in my scholastic career. I could name each one, describe how each inspired me, but such a task would fill over a hundred pages. My English teacher is one of the elite ten teachers who have taught me who I am, how to have and express opinions, how to challenge myself and others, and how to listen.

I aspire to become like these special teachers. I thank each and every one. Especially the passionate young man who taught me what it means to be a teacher.

I Learned How To Go On

by Melissa Knutson

A close friend of mine was supposed to come home Friday. He never came. He went from the hospital to heaven, Tuesday, he became an angel. Such an innocent, young life was taken due to complications of the heart. At school, all I could do was stare at Nolan's empty seat.

Miss Anderson, my teacher, talked to me for an hour after school before the wake. She told me about her personal experiences with loved ones dying and mentioned that I needed to go or I would regret it. She explained to me that God has a plan for everyone, and that He didn't want Nolan suffering anymore so He called for him. Miss Anderson told me I needed to talk to Nolan that night; that I needed to say my last good-byes. I didn't want to. I wanted my last image of Nolan to be the kid towering over everyone in the halls. Before I left for the wake, I received the biggest hug in the world from my teacher. Her hug lifted the weight off

I miss him so much...but, How can I say "Good-By"?

my shoulders and said that I will be alright; that I will get through the toughest confrontation of my life, thus far.

A few weeks had passed and I still hadn't visited Nolan's grave-stone. Miss Anderson questioned me why I had not. I couldn't answer. I broke down. I was ashamed of myself for not going. After softball practice one day, Miss Anderson dropped me off at Nolan's grave-site and drove around so I could talk to him. If it weren't for her, I don't think I would have ever gone. Miss Anderson knew how to teach me to cope and become a stronger person through my friend's death. She listened to me talk about our memories, lent a shoulder for me to cry on, and kept plenty of tissues in her room for me when I broke down. She treated me as a friend, not as a preacher, through the aftermath of Nolan's death.

One month after we lost Nolan, we were supposed to be all thrilled about our Junior Prom. I didn't think it was right to be having fun when a classmate of mine couldn't come to his Prom. Miss Anderson had a talk with me and showed me how she moved on after her fiance's murder. It then hit me. She was supposed to spend the rest of her life with this man she loved but his life was taken.

She is the perfect role model for today's youth. If she can move on and lead a life many envy, I can move on too. I went to the Prom and had a blast. Before I went to sleep that night, I thanked Nolan for all the memories and Miss Anderson for teaching me how to cope with the loss of my friend.

Realizing Through Hardship

by Ryan Lassabe

I t would be very easy to say that I attend a small school. In fact, I have had the same teacher for math and science for three years. This, however, has been a blessing and will likely affect my life's course, for this teacher is wonderful.

Her name: Dr. Leslie Wilson, Ph. D. in quantum chemistry, and I cannot begin to explain exactly what that means. One thing I do know is, this teacher has profoundly impacted not only my academic learning but my understanding of mankind. You see after much deliberation the time has come to choose my college major and after having an extraordinary experience with chemistry I have decided to devote my college experience to obtaining a degree in pharmacy.

It all started in my sophomore year when I was taking chemistry, a year ahead of my peers, and was left alone to defend myself against the upperclassmen. I didn't personally like any of them as I perceived them as rude and obnoxious, and obviously they didn't like me. I decided to put this hostile environment to good use and just completely focus on the subject at hand. Needless to say, with this motivation I got straight A's in chemistry, something done by only two others taking it that year. My teacher had motivated me in ways no other teacher had before. It wasn't just a push here or there. When I wanted to go further, she would take me to the side and teach me more than was needed. Soon, I loved chemistry and had great respect for this woman who could undoubtedly be making 3 times what our school had to offer.

This was actually the first time I was sad to see a subject end…EVER. Soon I found out I would be taking math with her the next year and was pleased enough with this. Anyway, as high school went on, you tend to forget how much you appreciate people. Junior year passed. I received A's and B's in math even with the distraction of my normal classmates. Then I received the wake up call I won't soon forget.

Senior year is half over and, as I walk into 1st period, there is a

The Lemonade Series

grim look upon my social studies teacher's face. Unsuspecting, he starts reading the announcements as usual and soon slows and looks up. "Dr. Wilson," he explains, "has been in a fire. As she was trying to escape from the second floor she had to jump from a balcony. Both her ankles are broken." My heart jumped, then went down and beat hard. I didn't want to hear this, and I didn't think it could be true. I had heard about the fire the night before but had no idea she lived in those apartments. I felt guilt as I remember being glad it wasn't me. Then he continued, "She lost over 10 years of research she had been doing." Apparently, unknown to us, she was working on another Ph. D. or something of that nature.

Ten days passed.

Well it's time for the good news. Dr. Wilson returned, wheel chair and all. She is now on crutches and is at this very moment recovering. She still teaches and doesn't like us to help her. She lives with friends and comes to work every day. (Yes, for the same pay.) That is someone I respect. That's dedication.

A Breath Of Fresh Air

by Catherine Lawhon

I am living proof of the impact a teacher can have on his/her student's life. I transferred from my private, Christian school to a public school when I was in sixth grade. I was accustomed to an environment where pants were not to be worn by girls, the "teachers pet" was the most popular person in the class, and co-education P.E. was strictly forbidden. Here, girls were wearing shorts, people threw paper at their teachers, and Lord have mercy—boys and girls had P.E. together! I was the scrawny new girl with a crooked smile, hand-me-down clothes, and a propensity for crying. I was too shy to try and start a conversation. Keep in mind, this was sixth grade; I wholeheartedly believed that the smallest faux-pas would ruin my life FOR-EVER. I was lonely and unhappy, but afraid to tell my parents about my situation because anything seemed better than going back to my old school and its oppressive rules. I stayed in the library during recess, shelving books to avoid being made fun of. Every once in a while, someone felt that it was their personal duty to leave an anonymous note on my desk, informing me of my status as a pariah, just in case I had not realized it on

"From the Other Side of the Desk"
Her love made me feel special!

my own. Although the spelling errors and mistakes in grammar are somewhat humorous to me now, ("no one wants you to be they're friend"), at the time, the letters were devastating, obliterating any infinitesimal bits of self-esteem I had built up shelving books in the self-help section of our library.

My homeroom teacher, Mrs. Kay McSwain, made all the difference in the world to me that year. Mrs. McSwain made me feel wanted in her classroom. The time I spent in her class everyday was a breath of fresh air. She always had fun, interesting ways of teaching a lesson. She told us that if we had anything we needed to talk about, we could confide in her. I will never forget how she looked at me right at that moment. Mrs. McSwain became more than just a teacher to me; she was my friend. She taught me that to make friends, I had to first be a friend to others. A few years earlier, Mrs. McSwain had written a book called, "From the Other Side of the Desk." She gave me a copy of it and on the inside cover wrote: "To Catherine, You'll always be someone special! Love you always, Mrs. McSwain" Mrs. McSwain inspired me to work hard in school and to never settle for less than my personal best. Six years, a set of braces, and a whole new wardrobe later, I have more friends than I could ever count and an acceptance letter and academic scholarship to the University of South Carolina. I attribute much of my happiness and success to the difference Mrs. McSwain made in my life.

Kindred Spirit

by Jessica Liptak

I remember the first time I heard the term kindred spirit. My seventh grade teacher told me I was hers. Never before had I felt as close to a teacher as I did to Mrs. Rago. She did more than educate—she served as my guide, my light through the dark tunnel I had encountered at the beginning of the year.

Aside from being understanding, Mrs. Rago also developed my strengths. I was and still am a heavy reader. Since we both had similar tastes in literature, she started recommending and loaning books to me. After a while, our exchanges turned into a sort of reading club as a few of my friends became interested in sharing stories. All of us got along quite well and we stayed in touch regularly during recess, sharing what we had read.

Along with encouraging my love for reading, my teacher also provided enrichment in the classroom. Unlike some of my other teachers, Mrs. Rago did not get upset when I went ahead of the class. Instead of seeing

Mirror, mirror on the wall—
It's my teacher,
though I'm short and she is tall!

a know-it-all trying to show off, she saw a bright student who just needed work that was a bit more challenging than the rest of the class could handle.

Our relationship moved beyond that of teacher and student. We were friends so alike in nearly all aspects that it was a wonder we were not related. From our short, thin hair to our view of the world, Mrs. Rago and I mirrored each other in nearly every way. We both loved dogs, and similar types of food. We were organized and opinionated. Our behavior, our reactions to certain things were also similar, more so than I could imagine.

I had been diagnosed with obsessive-compulsive disorder that year, better known as OCD. I was on medication and seeing a therapist, whom I wanted nothing to do with. It seemed like no one could understand what I was going through except Mrs. Rago. She, too, had suffered from OCD years ago. At the time, I was unaware of this. All I knew was that she did not think it was strange that I had to wash my hands after certain activities, or needed to keep things orderly. If I felt depressed at any time, she did not pressure me to talk, only listened when I felt ready to share my emotional burdens.

I owe my success as well as my recovery from OCD to this extraordinary, caring woman. Mrs. Rago went beyond standard education, strengthening me in mind and spirit. She saw me not only as a student, but also as a beautiful, intelligent person: her kindred spirit. She was a better listener than anyone I have ever known. She challenged me, allowed me to excel rather than holding me back with the rest of my class because she knew how I functioned. Without her, I would have been trapped in the tunnel with no one to light my way, unable to reach the end.

My Favorite Pair Of Underwear

by Keane Maddock

What kind of person qualifies as a "good" teacher? Then again, what is a "good" teacher? Is it an unconventional teacher? Is it a strict teacher? The truth is that a "good" teacher is like your favorite pair of underwear: personal, but not smothering; strict, but not too restricting. I was at the all-knowing age of fifteen. He was a grumpy old man of forty-five. These days, that does not sound like a perfectly healthy relationship with any human being.

My freshman year of high school started off with the death of my Grandpa, Louis. He was one of the greatest people I ever had the pleasure of knowing. He was a wonderful person with lungs the color of tar. He died of cancer. I began to look for answers. I tried everything from playing sports to juggling four girlfriends at one time. It seemed like these things just got me into more trouble. I was a terrible athlete, so I had no self-esteem and, amazingly, the girl-friends found out about one another. That was not pretty. Then, I walked into the Frankfort High School Theater. Wearing a pair of faded jeans and a tee shirt that should have put to death years ago was my favorite pair of underwear—Mr. Clossin.

He had a certain something about him that made you want to scream, "HERE'S MY LIFE—FIX IT!" Sure, he was a handy man at building sets, but being a handyman of life was his specialty. He put me in a world with no cares or worries through the magic of theater. Learning lines with singing songs became an everyday routine. I loved my new life. I learned something new everyday with him. I learned how to convey the inner-most thought of a character to the audience. I learned how to properly hang a spot light. I didn't know it then, but I was being taught how to deal with life. Mr. Clossin told me to never stop following my dreams. It is astonishing how little a teenager is told that. He became my personal backbone.

This once-in-a-lifetime relationship lasted for the next two years. He left during my junior year. He decided to pursue his dream of becoming a real actor. He left a legacy that would never be matched. Most importantly, he left the son he never had. Mike Clossin is now working on a movie called, "The Alamo." It is a big opportunity for him to do exactly what he wants to do. He is an actor. I am now following my dream of acting. I have been accepted to Ball State University and I will be majoring in musical theater.

Once again, I ask, what makes a "good" teacher? It is my teacher: Someone who is personal with me, someone that is strict when it is appropriate, and someone that has the experience and wisdom to help me in life. Mr. Clossin is my favorite pair of underwear.

Brick By Brick

by Erin Marcoe

I wasn't convinced that going there would change my behavior. I didn't believe that my experience there would be influential, that my life would drastically change. After participating in anorexia for two years, I was convinced there was no way anyone could bring about a change in me. I was determined not to let anyone interfere with the power and control the eating disorder had in my life.

Since my physical and mental health continued to deteriorate rapidly, my parents made the decision to have me admitted to an eating disorder clinic. My plan was to play by the rules, continue to conceal my emotions, and hopefully convince them I was recovered so they would send me home. I wouldn't allow myself to feel, I wouldn't allow anyone to get past my brick wall. No one could tear it down.

Every Monday morning I was expected to attend an education class. I wasn't motivated to be there. I figured this would be a great opportunity to sleep. I curled up on the couch, laying my head on one of the oversized pillows. My attention was captured when a tall man entered the room with a stack of papers. He was dressed casually, blond hair, and the thing I noticed the most was his face. It seemed very understanding and gentle. I quickly dozed off as the teacher began presenting his lesson. About two minutes after he started, my head jerked up in awareness. This teacher had just presented the topic of child abuse and as I sat up and started to listen, he continued on to mention how child abuse affects us in a way that we later develop eating disorders. I came to realize that his man wasn't here to teach us about government, mathematics, and English, but about life issues. Hearing another person talk about problems that I have been through, or I am faced with, hit my brick wall and a part of it began to crumble.

I became an attentive listener to Paul's lessons. He seemed to know me inside and out. He sensed my emotions that I so desperately tried to hide. He knew by the look in my eye when he talked about sexual abuse, depression, neglect, and self-mutilation. Not only did I listen to his lessons, but also I never skipped a class since that first day. Afterwards I would stay behind to talk with Paul; I confided in him. He listened to what I had to say. Paul helped me face my problems that I had run away from. I was afraid to deal with them, and Paul helped me overcome my fear, and face my problems. I knew it was the only way I could beat this disorder. I realized this wall would eventually have to come down brick by brick. I couldn't hide behind anorexia any longer, I had to fact it.

I will never forget the three months I spent at the Center For Chance. It did faze me; Paul influenced me in such a way that I lead a different life now. I can still remember that face of understanding and gentleness, and my mind goes to Paul whenever I am faced with a challenge.

Surprise yourself with a special treat to eat.

Dad's Lemonade Stand

Tips on Living with Love, Laughter and Lemonade!

Ode To Mrs. Renee Buchholz

by Barry Marquardt

My name is Barry Marquardt, and I now call myself a poet and a fan of literature. This is all thanks to my AP English teacher, Mrs. Renee Buchholz.

Before this year, I was one who resented reading. I hated reading. It took too long, it didn't entertain me, nor did it serve any purpose but to kill trees. When I first entered Mrs. Buchholz's class, I was introduced to the phrase "literary merit." She told us that works of "literary merit" were extraordinary books that not only told a story, but sent a timeless message that anyone can relate to. I was rather ignorant at the time. I thought: this is just an opinion, who says what books are better than others?

As the year progressed, our class read many works by various authors, like Henrik Ibsen, Nathanial Hawthorne, Arthur Miller, and everybody's favorite, Shakespeare. We also were able to choose two plays to read independently. The two I chose were by Arthur Miller, "All My Sons" and "The Crucible." As the second half of the year began, I became familiar with literature that I would never have read outside of this classroom. Through Mrs. Buchholz's teachings and the readings of these works, I saw what she meant months ago. I saw how reading can be so philosophical, inspiring and emotional. I felt sorry for characters that never existed. I felt these characters were real people, and their experiences were as real as my own. I learned to read, undertand, and have emotion for literature, and I finally understood how works are of "literary merit."

What Mrs. Buchholz truly inspired within me was poetry. At first, I was resentful of the analysis of poems. I felt poems were meant to be left for personal reading, and not to be dissected in a classroom. I thought poems aren't meant to have things forced out of them.

But through interpreting these poems, I came to a different perspective. I found that poets leave the work to us, to find our own meanings. They aren't meant to be read, then forgotten. Mrs.

The Lemonade Series

Buchholz inspired me so much that I have now begun to write my own poems independently. I never thought I could, because I am such a logical thinker. She brought creativity out of me and put within me an understanding of poetry and the poet's purpose for writing poems. I even wrote a poem that, as I write this now, has been advanced in a poetry competition and will be published in two poetry collections!

Mrs. Buchholz has inspired me to write and has taught me to understand. For this, she has made me a better person to the people around me as well as to myself, and to those who have left their works on earth for me to read and enjoy. To her, I am grateful.

The Inspiration To Think For Myself

by Melissa Marrero

In an age of political and ethical uncertainty, I found myself lost in a world that I was about to dive into, headfirst, toward an unclear future. As an avid history buff who was enchanted with the American ideal of justice, my college applications were sent off with my choice of a political science major clearly marked. Little did I know, however, how undecided I was as to my own views and beliefs on the issues that enshrouded my government. In a time where "Bombs over Baghdad" wasn't just an outcast song, I had no idea what I believed in. It was as if I was standing in darkness with an array of paths surrounding me. I didn't know which path to choose. It was then that I met my 12th grade American Government teacher, Mr. Geernaerdt. He soon became my flashlight. He brightened the complicated channels in my mind and let me choose for myself how I felt about certain issues. A flashlight lights the way but the holder must choose where to beam the light. That is exactly what Mr. Geernaerdt did for me.

Mr. Geernaerdt is one of those teachers who can make you understand ideas without you realizing that you are absorbing the lessons. His sarcastic and often cynical style caught my attention immediately and hypnotized me for the

> Now I can see the light! All I have to do is decide on where to beam it!

entire semester. He not only made my beliefs clear, he made me realize how passionate I could be. A skeptic might chalk this up to the fact that any civics teacher could have a tremendous influence on his student's opinions through the way in which he slants his lessons. Mr. Geernaerdt never had a hidden agenda though. He never even let us know how he felt about the topics we were discussing. In fact, the class even got into small debates over whether he was a liberal or a conservative. Mr. Geernaerdt was completely unbiased. For this I thank him because it allowed me to grow as an independent thinker and politician. The world would do well with more teachers like Mr. Geernaerdt because those who inspire independent thought inspire innovation. And innovation is what gets us into the future instead of leaving us a stagnant race.

   Mr. Geernaerdt is one of the most intelligent people I've ever met, and by far the most inspiring instructor. I ache for college now because of the passion within myself that he helped me to find. My mind is open. My pathways are bright and I have Mr. Geernaerdt, my flashlight, to thank for it. He not only taught me invaluable lessons, he let me discover myself. I am a stronger person because of this man, this teacher, who showed me what it was to formulate my own opinions. He set me free, and intellectual freedom is the greatest gift a teacher can give.

The Voice Of Love

by Lashanna Martin

When I was in third grade I met a teacher that changed my whole outlook on life. I attended a Catholic elementary school, and for the first half of my third grade year my teacher was a miserable woman named Sister Sebastian. But when the year was half over, all of the sisters were replaced with regular teachers. My class had the good fortune of being assigned Ms. Dietz, genuinely the most caring person I have ever met. Instead of yelling at us or finding reasons to constantly pick at our every move, she praised our good behavior and encouraged us to just be kids.

She instilled in us a love of reading that I still have today. I remember her reading, "Sarah Plain and Tall," and, "Bridge to Terabithia." Mostly, I remember reading, "The Lion, the Witch, and the Wardrobe," and decorating an entire wall of our classroom like the mystical land of Narnia. I remember that I always loved to hear her soft, sweet voice and that no matter how awful I might have felt, hearing her read always cheered me up.

I was especially lucky to have Ms. Dietz as a Sunday school teacher too. The only time I didn't put up a fight against going to school or church was when she was involved. Mrs. Dietz had a true gift for working with children. She made every kid feel loved and included. She never put anyone down and she would never stand by silently and watch anyone be hurt. She could make even the most stubborn kid eager to learn.

That summer, something dreadful happened. Ms. Dietz was killed in a freak accident saving one of the children she loved so much. We were told that she and a friend had stopped alongside a road to rest, leaving the other woman's child in the car just a few feet away. When the car started to roll away, Ms. Dietz rushed to stop it before any harm could come to the child inside. She did manage to rescue the child but she was not so lucky. She had been pressed between a guard rail and the car and had been too badly injured to survive. I was devastated when I heard the news, but I did learn

The Lemonade Series

something from her that I would never forget. What she taught my class was something more important than phonics or multiplication tables. She taught us to love and respect one another and ourselves. She taught us to love life and live it as best we could. But I learned something more than that. Because of Ms. Dietz, I learned of my own love for children. This fall I will start college and will be majoring in Elementary Education. I hope that someday I, too, can so selflessly dedicate myself to others and maybe even inspire another as she inspired me.

My Motivation

by Shaday Matthews

My all time favorite teacher was my seventh grade teacher, Ms. Spann. Although I am a high school junior, thus having many teachers between seventh and eleventh grade, she has had the biggest impact on my life.

When I was in the seventh grade, I didn't know what I wanted my life career to be like. But it wasn't until Ms. Spann's innovating teaching methods and "out-of-the-box" thinking that I felt hungry for knowledge. She taught Literature, which had started to become one of my least favorite subjects. In her class we read and did the other tasks that were required for a seventh grade English class. However, she always managed to put her own special twist to what we did and what we learned. No class day was ever the same. There was poetry, mock trials, dramatic sketches, writing short stories, and much more. But what really struck a passion inside of me was poetry. She gave me, along with others, the ability to express myself through words. Ms. Spann gave us the freedom of expression of our minds. Then, in the latter part of the year, all of her classes had to write skits and get into groups to form a plan to help change some of the ills of our communities. From each class one or two skits were selected from the topics underlined in the Civil Rights Movement. To my surprise, she chose my reading of the "Martin Luther King Birmingham Jail" scene. Being my first time ever writing something so major and having it chosen gave a boost of confidence within myself.

A few years later, from just that experience that instilled confidence, I have achieved much. That very next year I submitted a poem that I used to conclude my community improvement plan to Poetry.com in 2000, 2001, and 2002.

The experience and great opportunity that she gave me in writing a skit for performance purposes inspired me to write a one-act, thirty-page play that I submitted in the NAACP ACT-SO competition. I won the gold medal.

There is no doubt that she affected me as well as others. I would say she was the ultimate motivator in being creative in reaching students. Lastly, I thank her for all my success that I have had in Literature. I leave you with the poem that was inspired by Ms. Spann:

> To Change The World
> If we would start with one child,
> One soul,
> One spirit,
> One mind,
> One heart,
> We could change the world.
> If we could sing with one song,
> One melody,
> One harmony,
> One verse,
> One chorus,
> We could change the world.
> If we could start with this
> Universe,
> This earth,
> This country,
> This community,
> One corner,
> We have truly started to change
> the world little by little.

The World's Kindest Teacher

by Elizabeth McIlwain

Many years have passed and Mrs. Slay has moved away, but her love and compassion at a very scary time in my life remains with me. I was only seven years old when I was a student in Mrs. Slay's second grade class. I had lost my kidney transplant and was waiting for another kidney to be found for me. We did CAPD dialysis every night at home and I had to wear a little bag with a catheter in it all the time. I did not feel so great every day, but Mrs. Slay was kind and helpful no matter how I felt. She helped me with my math at her house in the afternoons and whenever she could. She knew that I wanted to stay with my class and not have to repeat a grade in school. I did not get the kidney until the third grade but Mrs. Slay was there to help me when I got home. We live in Alabama, but the transplant was done at the University of Minnesota. I had a really rough time and missed about half of the third grade. When I got home, Mrs. Slay made sure I got all my missed work done. I went onto the fourth grade with my class. I am now graduating in a few weeks and I want to be a Child Life Therapist to work with chronically ill children. I know how much it means to a sick child to have someone help them succeed in school. Her love and encouragement at a very scary time in my life made a huge impact on me. I have heard that she named her baby after me, Anna Elizabeth. What a huge honor! I know her Anna Elizabeth will sail through life with such a loving mother.

The Lemonade Series

An Unknown Blessing

by Jasmin Mercedes

I've had several teachers who have inspired me in my life, but none as great as Mr. Ruth. I first met Mr. Ruth my freshman year in high school, and now I am on my way to my senior year and off to college. I'll never forget the days I felt I should give up and when I was actually considering dropping out. I did horribly in grammar school and I didn't think I was smart enough to make it to graduation. Almost everyone in my family had dropped out of high school and they expected me to be the only one to "make it" to show that there was still some sense left in our family. I had asked myself, "Why should I have to work for their mistakes?" or "I can just get my GED." I felt that I needed some guidance when in reality I was searching for someone to just agree with me. No one else seemed to care. I spoke to my guidance counselor, some friends, and even a neighbor and no one thought of it as such a big deal.

Here's where Mr. Ruth comes in. One day, one of the not-so-smart students hadn't come to school. Students gasped when he told us that she had dropped out that very day. I, on the other hand, wasn't too shocked. I could almost see tears in Mr. Ruth's eyes as he spoke. He said to us, "You know, it breaks me apart when I hear about things like this. What could have been going on with her that would make her do such a thing? I'm pretty sure that no one in here is going through what I went through growing up…" Mr. Ruth told us a long and sad story about his past which gave me a pain in my heart. He grew up a very poor boy with 4 younger brothers and a sister, and was forced to build his own bicycles and eat the same old oatmeal everyday. His father left his family when he was 9 years old. He respected and loved his mother dearly and refused to ask her for the little she had. It felt like Mr. Ruth was talking to me. At the end of class, I gave him a tight hug and said, "Thank you for everything, Mr. Ruth." He smiled at me and looked confused, but I walked away before he could ask me any questions. It was then that my mind was changed forever. I will be attending college and studying Anesthesiology. Though he doesn't know it, he has truly been a blessing to me and everlasting inspiration for my soul.

Lesson Of Life

by Tanya Methven

My teacher Mr. Rigsbee told us that he had been very sick. He said he thought he was going to die. He told us he thought he had cancer and was going to get tested later that week. So he said it was time to teach us all a lesson about life.

He grouped us up and gave us huge glass jars with a bunch of items to fit inside, ranging from large objects and books, to pebbles, sand, and water. He said the jar represented our life, and the objects represented things inside our lives. The object of the exercise was to fit as many things into the jar as possible. Every group crammed as much in as possible and some got further than others did, but no one was able to fit all the items in the jar.

"Why can't you fit everything into your lives?" One student answered, "There's no more room." Another said, "Everyone's jar is full, but some people did fit more objects in than others."

Mr. Rigsbee said, "Every one of these items can fit into one of these jars, it is possible. The problem is your priorities."

How did he fit everything in, and I couldn't?!

The Lemonade Series

Mr. Rigsbee grabbed an empty jar and took the largest objects and began setting them into the jar. "You've got to take the biggest things in your life and make them first. All the different aspects of your life are not random, they are hierarchial, all ranked by importance." He kept putting the largest of the objects left to be put in. By the time the jar appeared full, the things he had left to put in were the pebbles which filled the little cracks. Then he added the sand, which filled the cracks in the pebbles and finally the water, which filled any space of air there was left in the jar. "And that is how you can fit everything into your lives."

That lesson made me think a lot about my own values and the things that are the most important to me. I started prioritizing those "big" things first and found that I was a lot more efficient that way. Mr. Rigsbee's cancer hypothesis was unfortunately correct, even though no one knows how he suspected it. The cancer was in several of his organs around his liver, which I guess was a very rapid growing cancer, and he died a little over two months after he found out he had it. He still taught for about a week after he was diagnosed to say his goodbyes and to eliminate stress from his life. However, in that week my Humanities class and I witnessed a whole new set of values in this man. To me, my biggest priority was success and education; to him, his biggest was to squeeze the last drops of meaning out of life, to make the biggest difference he could make, and to touch one last heart. I realized that these priorities are quite different in size, and meaning, with each of us making those choices in our lives.

Uncle Pete

by Megan Minkow

It was first period, the first day of high school, the first day I had met this man. He was intimidating, pacing back and forth, telling us in a stern voice what he expected from us when delving into literature, ranging from *The Odyssey* to *Gulliver's Travels*. Mr. Ives was threatening to some, but to me, he proposed challenges. English being my favorite class, I would not let him ruin my joy for literature with his grumpiness. I felt Mr. Ives was putting on the façade of the stern intellectual; my friends and I loved to mock him and catch him off-guard. He joked back with us. Mr. Ives and I became friends—he knew I didn't take him all too seriously (except when instructing us of course).

Mr. Ives, or "Uncle Pete" as we came to call him, asked if any of us wanted to write movie reviews for the school newspaper, The Trinity Voice. I found this to be a great opportunity, and immediately went for it. I found reviews to be a lot of fun. I saw movies, got to voice my opinion about them, and even got my picture in every issue! Mr. Ives guided me in my critiques; this further helped me in writing great analytical papers. Moreover, I got to know him, and he got to know me.

In my sophomore year, I signed up for his newspaper class to become an "official" writer of The Trinity Voice. When it was time to select editors, I told Mrs. Ives I wanted to be one. I told him, although I was the youngest of the class, I was up for the challenge. To my surprise, he selected me as the Arts & Entertainment Editor; the youngest ever for The Trinity Voice. He trusted me—he knew I was a good writer, and he knew of my interest in the arts. Mr. Ives gave me a quick lesson in what it means to be a journalist and I learned new approaches to writing.

Since joining The Trinity Voice team, I have expanded my writing talents to The Orlando Sentinel's Flipside!, a weekly entertainment product of The Orlando Sentinel that is written for, by, and about Central Florida high school students. I am honored to have been on

The Lemonade Series

this team for two years, and love to hear people commenting on my writings knowing that over 1,500,000 people read my words.

Mr. Ives isn't just a teacher or a mentor, he is a pal. I don't just talk to him about school, but I talk to him about politics, life, and family. I am grateful to Mr. Ives to have given me my start at The Trinity Voice, where I am now editor-in-chief. Mr. Ives truly has had a significant impact on the way I look at the world, and has taught me to question all that surrounds me—just like any good journalist should do.

The Teacher Who Never Leaves My Side
by Christina Molino

Honestly, I was never a popular kid among the other students. A major reason was that, instead of caring about what I looked like on the outside, I cared more about how I did in school. In my sophomore year of high school, I decided to transfer into the Camden County Technical Schools for their Allied Health Program. Of course, I was extremely nervous about starting a new school. However, those nerves were calmed when I met Mrs. Lee. I do not know what it was about this teacher, but something in her eyes made me feel safe and comforted. Sure, it is a teacher's job to help their students any way they can inside the classroom. Mrs. Lee was different, because she also helped me outside of the classroom a number of times. Whenever I was having a problem at home with my parents, I would go to her. It was Mrs. Lee who convinced me, despite the fact that I had no date, that I should still go to my Junior Prom.

On May 15, 2002, the worst thing ever happened to me. My mother was killed at the McDonalds where she worked when a man decided to drive through the store. Before I called anyone, other than family, I called Mrs. Lee at school. Although she was busy teaching, she took the time to try to calm me down over the phone. When school ended, she drove from Pennsauken to Mount Ephraim to sit with me at the crash site. I could tell that she wanted me to talk about my feelings, but she did not pressure me. At the funeral, I told her that I blamed myself, because I had a fight with my mom the night before her death. I will never forget the words that she said to me after I told her that. She said, "Chris, I never want to hear you say that again. Because it is not your fault that some idiot did this." Since I missed almost three weeks of school following her death, I had a great deal of work to make up when I returned. Still confused and grieving, I never let my grades slip. Until December, when I moved to Texas, I always talked to Mrs. Lee about anything and everything. When she was absent most of the week leading up to my final day in

The Lemonade Series

New Jersey, I thought I would never get to say goodbye to her. However, I went to school on my last day, and there she was, in tears. We promised to keep in touch, and both of us have and, will always, keep our end of the bargain. Mrs. Lee was more than a teacher; she is a great friend that I can turn to, no matter what. That is why I know she will never leave my side, no matter what state we are in.

When something doesn't go your way, laugh and look the other way.

Dad's Lemonade Stand

Tips on Living with Love, Laughter and Lemonade!

Daddy I Found You

by Grace Monrian

When a teacher loves their job,
There is not any care
Whether students understand;
When a teacher loves their students,
They do not care for their student's learning,
But gives grades;
When a teacher who loves them both,
They help their students succeed.
But the one who lives for their students
Loves to teach, help, spend time,
And is there when the time counts.

Students never feel more alone than in transition years. Love shown to a student by a teacher can inspire education for a lifetime. Music teachers have a special opportunity of influence for four years. Michael McQuerry allows each student to call him the personal nickname, "Mr. Mac," and testifies to his ability to discern music, laugh and inspire.

As I struggled though my awkward high school years, I discovered how much a teacher can care. An excelling student overloads themselves at the chance of exceeding set expectations. Normally I was an excelling student, but at this point I did not have any hope for my future, and could not associate with my loved ones. I could not sleep, concentrate, control emotions; I had experienced hyperventilation, sweats and panic attacks. Mac related family instances and helped me comprehend my chemical imbalance, which a doctor's diagnosis verified later.

One of the biggest struggles of my life was overcoming my father's homosexuality. His non-parent-know-how turned me into his 1920s mom for six years. When he found a match I was allowed to run free with punishments for nonexistent problems he mentally created. Mac could see in my eyes the problems that persisted as I struggled in faith. His constant hope allowed me to see God's hands.

The Lemonade Series

Through this experience I would be able to accept, connect with, and encourage many different types of people. My faith thrived and I decided to be a missionary. I gained faith in good men through him. True love is someone who is willing to be there in torturous times.

I am now a 4.0 student with advanced classes living at my mom's. I design sets, work a part-time job; I am a hired artist, worship leader, mentor, planning to firefight and attend college. My confidence and love for life is contagious. Without Mr. Mac's guidance and vocal training, I would not be able to perform my personal ministry.

My mother refers to Mac as my third Dad, for being my best father model. The best thing about being a teacher is the opportunity to be a parent to thousands of students. Every year his self-sacrifice is to run the LA Marathon fund-raiser for choirs at age 56 after having two heart surgeries, which teaches perseverance. Mac takes situations and molds each student's morals to grow each year to new heights. This is one who shall be a great daily loss. The moral lessons I have received from him are with me each day as I grow in my faith. Wherever you are is your mission field by his example.

He Believes In Me

by Cherry Mun

At school, I was always the recluse that nobody cared to acknowledge. I believed that my existence on earth was futile because I had nothing to offer to this world. I did not have a talent; I was not skinny or pretty; I was not gifted with intelligence, either. Simply, I lacked confidence and self-esteem. I was just a hard-working, mediocre student with hushed dreams. Eventually, I reached the point where I would contemplate suicide almost every day. At the tender age of thirteen, I had already devised a method to end my life. I thought that nobody would suspect anything. But, I was wrong.

Mr. Reed, my eight grade English teacher, had suspected that something was troubling me. He pulled me out of his class one day to confront me about his suspicions. He asked me if I was feeling suicidal. At first, I was too shocked and embarrassed to respond. Then, after a brief moment of getting over the shock and embarrassment, I quietly said, "Yes. How did you know?" First, I was surprised to learn that Mr. Reed had figured me out by reading the essays that I had written in his class. Then, I was surprised to learn that he had taken time out of his busy schedule to read my writing. For the first time, I felt as though I had a voice.

My state of mind, as well as my perspective on life, had changed that eventful morning outside his classroom door. Mr. Reed, with sincerity and compassion in his eyes, had said to me, "I want you to always remember that I believe in you, so don't you even think about leaving this earth because I care. And, because I believe that you have so much to offer to this world. You have potential, Cherry. You are compassionate, intelligent, and hard-working. We need people like you." Tears were rolling down my face as he said this because I knew that he had turned my life around in as little as ten minutes. He had reached out to me, not only as my teacher, but as a caring human being. I would never forget him and his words of hope and inspiration.

The Lemonade Series

Four years have passed since I was in eighth grade. I have been through a lot in my trying teenage years. However, I do not think that I could have gotten to where I am today, if it were not for Mr. Reed. Even though some people say that I am not smart enough to be a doctor, I am not discouraged from pursuing my dream of becoming a pediatrician because I know that I will always have the support of Mr. Reed. Wherever I go and whatever I do, I know that somebody believes in me. I am grateful to have met a teacher who did more than fulfill his duties as a teacher.

Accent On Success

by Doris Oghor

The ultimate goal of most teachers is to increase a student's knowledge and skills. Many teachers, however, do not limit themselves to impacting only knowledge. They are able to recognize teens in trouble emotionally, and help to nurture and heal them. In the process, they effect profound changes in the lives of these teens, and leave an indelible impression in their minds. My fifth grade teacher, Mrs. Alexander, was one such teacher.

In April 1997, I transferred from a middle school in Nigeria to an intermediate school in Houston, Texas. I was miserable in my first week in school. I had no friends and could not fully comprehend what everyone was saying. People spoke too fast for me to understand and I had an accent that alienated many. Very soon the word had gone out that there was a new African girl in the fifth grade. Students would ask me questions like, did you live in the jungle and sleep in trees? Were you not afraid to sleep around wild animals at night? How come you are able to speak English? How did you come to America? Are you here to attend school because there are no schools in Africa? The questions were unending and very insulting. Students would congregate to laugh at and tease me. When it came time for me to read and I stumbled on certain words, the entire class would erupt into thunderous laughter. I would choke on words and prayed that the ground would open up and swallow me. God, I would ask, what have I done to merit this humiliation? I spent most of my time in the restroom hiding from my tormentors. I invented different excuses to keep from going to school.

Several weeks later, I was moved into a different class where I met my angel, Mrs. Alexander. In her class, she talked about diversity, differences in culture and language, respect for all beings and tolerance for people that are different from us. Her words were very reassuring and uplifting. For the first time, I felt relieved and happy that there was someone who could understand my predicament. I summoned up the courage and told her my problems. She was very supportive. She encouraged me to ignore the ignorant bullying kids and to always remember that I was special. She would stay after school to help with my reading problems. I could not have survived the fifth grade without her support and love. With her constant tutoring and advice, I began to notice some changes in myself. I became bold, happy and stopped having suicidal thoughts and ideas of running away from home. My circle of friends increased, my grades went up, my self-esteem soared tremendously, and school became a fun place to be at. Indeed, Mrs. Alexander sowed in me the seeds of learning, love and respect; attributes that changed my life forever. She will always be my hero.

Mr. Mooney

by Erin Olshever

As Eleanor Roosevelt once said, "Many people will walk in and out of your life, but only true friends will leave footprints on your hearts." Ironically enough, Mr. Mooney has been one of those select few who has left an everlasting imprint in my life.

Walking into Mr. Mooney's class the first day of school was a shock when I noticed he was in a wheelchair; Mr. Mooney is a paraplegic. Mr. Mooney taught class every day ignoring what he knew others were saying about him, and always taught to his full potential, educating me on life. His laid back teaching style helped us feel comfortable. Coming to his class ever day reminded me that I needed to relax.

There are no regrets in life... Everything happens for a good reason!

This past year has been particularly difficult for me. Recently I was diagnosed with IBS. What I hoped was just a stubborn stomach ache was permanent. I befuddled doctors since I have the rarest form of the syndrome, the type that less than one percent of the population has. I didn't feel very well with this diagnosis. One of the major causes of IBS is stress, and I was caught in a catch-22: my IBS was intensified by stress, and stress was a major trigger of my IBS. It is a vicious cycle that I am still working on breaking, since being sick nearly every day was taking quite a toll on me—I was often paralyzed by pain.

On a day when I was at my worst, Mr. Money saw me during a free period to ask if I could help him. For a moment I just stared at him in wonder. Even when I was doubled over in pain, I felt too awkward to ask someone for help. I quickly shook off my amazement and said, "Yes." Mr. Mooney has since often asked me to do him favors; I know there is less than a handful of people whom Mr. Mooney even asks.

I have never believed in coincidences, everything happens for a reason. Mr. Mooney doesn't know about my health problems, and has no idea that asking me to assist him with something was actually doing me an even greater benefit. Mr. Mooney has served as an inspiration. He not only recovered from an extremely serious accident that left him paralyzed, but he lives his life so that he has no regrets. He doesn't let little things stop him, and is never afraid to ask for help. If he can recoup from whatever did happen to him, then I have no excuse not to accept and deal with my IBS.

Mr. Mooney has proven to me that I can conquer anything. Nowadays, the word hero is often overused. Once, it meant someone who stood out above the rest and served as a role model, teaching others how to better live and enjoy life. Mr. Mooney exemplified never taking a single day of life for granted. Mr. Mooney is a true hero!

Care Spelled, Carr

by Roxanne Parker

April 3, 2002 was just another ordinary Wednesday for me. There were dark circles under my eyes from not getting any sleep the night before, and my appearance was nothing to be proud of. That horrible thing doctors call depression was again taking over my life. I was rapidly losing weight, not sleeping, and exercising all the time. I was sick of taking pills that didn't make me feel any better. I was sick of pretending that I felt great. Most of all, I was sick of being a burden to my family. They always told me they loved me and said they wanted to help, but I just felt like they were saying it because they felt obligated. I decided that is was time to take matters into my own hands and make things better for everyone. I would be alone when I got home from school, with access to a gun.

I sat in my morning classes like a zombie. I kept thinking of how much easier life would be for my mom if I were gone. She had gone through so much because of me the past year. I wanted to end her suffering more than my own. When I started to leave English class, Mrs. Carr grabbed me before I could get out the door. She wanted to know if I would come in after school. I said I would come back with no real intention of actually doing it. I'm not sure why, but I did go talk to Mrs. Carr after school was over. Mrs. Carr showed me my grade. It was a D-. I was normally an A student. She turned to me, looked me in the eye, and said, "Roxanne, how does my best student drop to this in a few short weeks?" I'll never forget what happened next. I started to cry and Mrs. Carr pulled me into her arms. She told me that she cared and that if I ever needed anything that she would be there. Mrs. Carr even gave me her phone number and said that I could call her anytime I wanted.

When I left Mrs. Carr's classroom that day I felt like a different person. I realized if a teacher cared, how much more did my own mother care? Thinking about killing myself was selfish and cowardly. Anyone can take their own life, but it takes a strong person to rise up

The Lemonade Series

to life's challenges. I finally got the courage to seek the help I needed and to talk to my parents about how my life was going.

In August of 2002 my senior year started. I was voted my high school's 2002 homecoming queen. In just a few short months my life was turned around and I was truly feeling great. I will never forget what Mrs. Carr did for me on that ordinary day in April. Teachers deserve more credit. After all, Mrs. Carr was just doing her job, but my life was changed forever.

His Eyes Twinkled With Care

by Betsy Potter

In my three years in high school I have had a lot of teachers. Some I enjoyed and some it took a while for me to connect with. Although I still have college to look forward to, I doubt I will ever find a teacher as unique and special as my Spanish teacher, Senor Metz.

When I started my junior year of Spanish and found out I would have Metz for a teacher, I was a little intimidated. He was known for being a tough, but very good teacher, and I wondered if I had made the right choice to stay enrolled in the course.

The way that Senor has influenced me personally came at a time when I really needed someone. I loved to dance for as long as I can remember. When I became involved in the dance squad at my school, I was thrilled. I was hooked and every season I participated by dancing at football and basketball games beside my friends. The day came my senior year when I would

Please...please... all I really want is to make the dance team!

The Lemonade Series

walk to the bulletin board to see if I had made the team. I was so excited to see who made the team and I was thinking of all the things we could accomplish in the upcoming season. I was devastated to find that I had not made the team. I was in shock as I walked to my first hour of the day - dance class. I passed Senor as I walked through the hallway and he jokingly asked, "Didn't make it, did you?" Through my tears I answered, "No I didn't." Senor's face dropped and he instantly knew I wasn't kidding. I kept walking but I found out later that he had stopped one of my friends later in the hall to see exactly what happened and if I was alright. All day people tried to console me but nothing worked. I didn't understand what happened. Then came Spanish class. The minute I walked into class Senor took me out into the hall and said to me, "I am so sorry. I know how much dancing means to you and I know that it was not because of your talent. You are a beautiful dancer and one of the best out there. If you ever need anything you can talk to me." And then he walked back into the room. That's all he said, yet because it came from Senor, it meant so much more. It meant something that he took notice of my individual talent. The rest of the day I was still upset, yet I knew that I had connected with Senor and he cared.

That's the kind person Senor is. Looking back, I want to thank Senor for not only teaching me Spanish, but teaching me what it is like to reach beyond what your job requires of you and caring for your students like you would your own children.

The Teacher Who Inspired Me To Change My Life

by Eric Pouliot

My choice for a teacher who has inspired me in a positive way is not only a teacher but a great friend, Mr. Belanger. He is a man of his word and loyal to all the students. Mr. Belanger influences his pupils in that he respects, trusts and interacts with them. Mr. Belanger is a Shop teacher at Southbridge High School, and his positive attitude has affected me in all of my subjects and life.

He changed my life by making me realize that there is more to life then just fun and games, and that your going to have to get serious someday. During one of our discussions he recommended a college that he thought would be of interest to me. I had no idea what direction I was going to take after graduation. I researched the school and realized that this would be the best choice for my future after high school. The college was New England Tech. I enrolled today!

The heart that he wore on his sleeve was for all to see, and he wasn't shy about his past. There was not one bit of remorse or regret in this man. He would tell us stories about himself or his family that would help us when we might have been in a pickle with our problems. This helped me in a positive way by realizing everything happens for a reason and that you should make the best of the moment at hand. We had both shared a death in the family last year, his father and my grand father. We shared our feelings about our losses, and I was able to see how he dealt with the situation. That had an enormous impact on me by seeing how he had dealt with it.

A role model but also a friend, Mr. Belanger is a man who I can look up to, but at the same time I can also relate to, because he isn't just a teacher to his students but a great friend. In a time where most role models might be your favorite musical artist, Mr. Belanger is the person that any adult or student can come up to and find a kind-hearted, smart and friendly man where nothing is unappreciated, only respected and dignified.

Mr. Belanger has more than inspired me to change my life in a positive way; he has changed every life he has ever come in contact with. He is a blessing to this world, a man with such pure intentions he should be awarded teacher of the century! I also truly believe that Mr. Belanger might just have a little more faith in us than everyone else, so that is why I have chosen Mr. Raymond Belanger as the teacher that has most inspired me to change my life.

Kind Words And A Gentle Heart
by Jenni Rainey

I was in the sixth grade when I first met her. We lined up outside the big doors on the black top. I was surrounded by friends and was ready to begin a new year of school. Little did I know this school year would teach me many lessons, and my teacher would leave a footprint on my heart forever. I remember walking into Mrs. Miller's sixth grade class and being amazed. It was unlike any of my other class rooms. Instead of posters of animals and different things plastered on the wall, I remember seeing quotes, or posters of people such as Martin Luther King, Jr. I remember hearing her gentle voice as we walked in her room, making sure she greeted each of us.

Even with my father's death,
Her encouragement makes me smile
And believe in tomorrow.

We started learning immediately. One of my favorite things to do in Mrs. Miller's class was have to Read-A-Thons. This is

The Lemonade Series

where you got to read ALL day long but you got to bring in your sleeping bag, or bean bag, and food! We would move all the desks to the side of the room and set up "camp" so to speak. Read-A-Thons were always fun days!

The year was soon to come to a close. We began a poetry unit which at first I didn't really like, but as time went on it became my favorite part of the day. I would go in during recess, or before school to have Mrs. Miller look over my poetry. She taught me so much, but most of all she taught my heart how to speak. It was the beginning of May, school would be out soon, and I was excited. Summer was just around the corner, and I couldn't wait—until I received the bad news. It was May 2nd, and I was told my father had died. This was devastating to me. I didn't know what to think. How was I suppose to live without my daddy? I missed about a week of school. When I returned, my classmates had gotten a rose bush for me, and a card. (The rose bush still blooms every spring!) Mrs. Miller was the most welcoming. When I re-entered class she was standing there with her arms open. I didn't deal with my father's death very well, except through poetry. It is because of Mrs. Miller, and her teaching me how to let my heart speak that I was able to overcome that time in my life. I still write poetry today, and I have even had three poems published. Every time I finish a poem, I think of her. I think of her kind words and her gentle heart that poured into the lives of her students. I think of Mrs. Miller and how she taught my heart to speak, and for that I will be forever grateful!

"Some people come into our lives, leave footprints on our hearts, and we are never the same."
   -Anonymous

The Story Of Jessica
by Jessica Reeder

I remember when I was in the third grade, there was this girl who had a very hard time, and I watched our teacher, Mrs. Petersen, help her. I will never forget the way that those two connected the first time they met. I could just feel in my heart that they were instant friends. This girl that I'm talking about now, her name was Jessica, and her life wasn't that great. She had two parents like everybody else. Her father and her mother got a divorce when she was six years old. Her father made a lot of stupid mistakes to ruin his life, and part of her childhood. He drank, and did drugs. He would drag her along everywhere he went, whether it was to court so that the judge wouldn't send him to jail, or to his friend's house to smoke marijuana. I could never tell whether something was wrong with her because she hid it so well. That is what some people said, but I think it was because of this teacher who helped her through it all. Mrs. Petersen was there for Jessica from the very beginning and still is today. I remember there were many times when Jessica needed Mrs. Petersen's help, but there was one time that was extremely important.

Jessica's father took her to Mexico with him to see the woman who is now her step-mother. They got married while in Mexico, and then he left Jessica in Mexico, with her step-mother. When Jessica's grandparents sent for her to come back to school, she had already missed three months. Mrs. Petersen worked with her for many hours to get her grades up, and to make sure she passed the third grade. Because of Mrs. Petersen's help, Jessica became a better person.

Mrs. Petersen has changed schools, and now teaches first grade at Majestic Elementary in Utah. Jessica still goes today to see how her friend and second mother is doing. The reason I know so much about these two is that I was that little girl.

My name is Jessica K-yong Reeder. I am now sixteen, and I have been adopted by my grandparents. My life was really bad when I was younger. I never showed it because I just don't talk about those things even now. I thought that this was the time to though, because I have the opportunity to tell you what a wonderful person my teacher and friend is. She has helped me to become everything I am today. Who knows what would have happened if I didn't have anybody that cared enough to help me along the way. She has changed my life; she showed me how wonderful life can truly be. I'm glad that I had the privilege of knowing her. There is a saying, "only one in a million." Mrs. Petersen is the one in a million for me; I guess she was my miracle as I grew up.

The Teacher Who Taught Me To Make Lemonade From Lemons
by Cynthia Roth

Mrs. Modzelewski. Imagine being a sixth grader and seeing a name on your schedule you would have to practice saying all summer. I never would have guessed how someone with such a frightful name would have such a kind heart.

With the sound of my alarm clock, I knew the day I had been anticipating finally arrived…my first day in Valley Stream North Junior/Senior High School! My name was not on any of the attendance rosters because of late registration, and my teachers appeared to be annoyed at this inconvenience. Luckily, I then encountered Mrs. Modzelewski. When I explained that my name was not on the attendance list, she smiled, and said, "It's okay, just take a seat and we'll take care of it." Despite my one pleasant encounter, I feared going back to school. Every morning I would lie in bed with butterflies in my stomach wishing I could run away.

133

Eventually, I was diagnosed with a phobia of school, and my counselor suggested that I talk to Mrs. Modzelewski. When I walked into her room that afternoon, she was sitting at a desk, surrounded by students, with her long black hair flowing down her back, and her dark brown eyes were tearing from laughter. As I approached her, she looked up, revealing her gentle welcoming smile. She offered me a seat, and said, "I'm here to help you. If you need anything, I'll get it for you. Except a new car. I can't even get myself a new car." Mrs. Modzelewski always made me feel welcome by inviting me back to chat with her after school, and each day I became more eager to go to school so that I could hang out with her. Finally, I no longer feared going to school because I knew that if anything happened, Mrs. Modzelewski would be there. She also helped to build my self-esteem throughout the years, giving me the courage to run for senator of my grade. Although I lost the first time, I ran again the following year and I won! I never would have had the courage to run for office before I met Mrs. Modzelewski.

Currently, I am finishing my junior year and Mrs. Modzelewski continues to listen to me and offer me advice. Looking back, I realize how Mrs. Modzelewski has affected me, and how the actions of one exceptional woman changed the course of my life. Although I have aspired to be a lawyer since third grade, I am considering a teaching career, so that I may inspire others just as Mrs. Modzelewski inspired me. By teaching me to make the best of what life hands you, Mrs. Modzelewski has taught me to make lemonade from lemons, a lesson I will never forget. Now that I have known Mrs. Modzelewski for five years, I realize she is not the "frightful" person I thought she was when I saw her name on my seventh grade schedule…she is my hero.

A Wonderful Ride Through Life
by Leah San Agustin

A very special teacher influenced my life at the hardest point in my life, which I am eternally grateful for. Mrs. Mills was my sixth grade teacher at Whittier Christian Schools. She cared for all of her past and present students in and out of the classroom. She was known for her funny lessons and great smile. Her humor came to shine through her genuine love as a teacher. When I was twelve, my parents were in a nasty divorce. My sister I were victims of my father's anger. My sister was born with a developmental disability, and today is scarred from these memories. One day in April, my mother had told me that she needed to have open heart surgery really soon and had a fifty-fifty chance of survival. I was in tears when she told me. The first person I thought of was my sister. Who would we live with, and how I would ever get to college. This was on top of dealing with the divorce. I spent many nights crying and trying to ask God why He let things happen like this to me. I was forced to grow up and become an adult while other kids worried about coloring pictures. I began to take on responsibilities that astonished many children and adults around me. I became mature and strong despite the situation. Mrs. Mills saw that I had no one to turn to in my situation. She became a help to me in expressing my feelings about the situation. I had also been made fun of and had to deal with a lot of false gossip. Mrs. Mills also knew that my mom could not drop off and pick me up from school, because her recovery time would be three months. She became my permanent ride to and from school. Mrs. Mills had told me that her father had the same surgery. She calmed my worst fears, and was the first person who understood how difficult this was for me. I remember when I first saw my mother after her surgery and cried, because I couldn't understand any of the madness I was involved with. As I sat next to my mom's bed, I couldn't help but remember how Mrs. Mills had always told me that God is with us to help us when we can't help ourselves. Now that it has been four years since my mother's surgery, I look back and see how much Mrs. Mills' kindness has inspired me to show my genuine love for people in trying to do whatever I can to make their work situations better. Mrs. Mills also got me to start smiling no matter what situation I was in, because things could always be worse. If there was anything I could say to Mrs. Mills again, I think I would tell her that she impacted my life and will forever be remembered in my heart with a smile.

Remind Me
by Kathryn Semple

You remind me of reality
When I'm feeling sad
You remind me of good
When things have gone bad

You remind me of independence
When I want to follow
You remind me of my worth
When it's my pride I have to swallow

You remind me of freedom
When I feel surrounded
You remind me of flying
When my wings are grounded

You remind me of music
When I only hear noise
You remind me of dancing
When I've lost my poise

You remind me of the start
When all I see is black
You remind me of kindness
When manners start to slack

But most of all
You remind me of you
With the way that you are
And the things that you do

This poem is written about my Humanities teacher, Mrs. McCray.

The Lemonade Series

She is such a strong and intelligent woman. She has an excellent way of explaining complicated, philosophical concepts so that not only do her students understand them, they expand on them. She has a wonderful presence and she has influenced me to look at new experiences with an open mind, and to be aware of the world around me. I am so thankful that I could experience her teaching and I could only hope that others can benefit from her dedication and knowledge as I have.

Let a special person know how very special they are.

Dad's Lemonade Stand

Tips on Living with Love, Laughter and Lemonade!

Mrs. Thomas
by Misty Snyder

When I was in second grade, I was diagnosed with Tourette Syndrome. No one in my family knew much about it or even what it was. My mom is a CAN, so she did some research on it to figure out what it was that I had. At the time, Mrs. Sandy Thomas was my teacher. She was wonderful about everything. She met with the school board and the principal to keep me in school. The principal wanted to pull me out of school because he didn't have knowledge of what Tourette Syndrome was. Mrs. Thomas didn't want me to be pulled out of class. She wanted me to stay right where I was. We didn't have assigned seats that were arranged alphabetically then. We were able to sit whereever we wanted to, but we had to sit in the same seat everyday. I chose to sit up front because I loved to learn. When my "ticks" started to come out, people were asking me why I was doing that. Since I couldn't control it, the only answer I could say was, "I don't know why I'm doing it." Mrs. Thomas saw what was going on, so she moved me to the back of the classroom so no one could see my ticks coming out. She talked to me and told me that if I would ever need to just get up and walk around, then I could go out in the hall. She never questioned me about my actions because she knew that they were uncontrollable. I can re-member hating that I had Tourette Syndrome because I thought people would make fun of me and I still do today at certain times, but I have learned and realized that having Tourette Syndrome makes me who I am. Mrs. Thomas made me understand that it's something that I will always have and nothing can ever change that. I have learned to deal with this by having people help me understand what it is and what I can do to help it. Mrs. Thomas is the person who gave me strength to get through the tough times when my ticks were really bad. To this day, not many people know what Tourette Syndrome is, and many of those other people mistake it for something else. I am considered to be a handicaped child in my school district, but I don't look or feel like it. I don't want to be treated differently than anyone else. All I ever wanted is to be treated fairly and for people not to look at what I have, but to look at the person who I am and not judge things on what they are unaware of. Mrs. Thomas would never let us judge people and that is the greatest value that I have ever learned from my greatest teacher.

I Have Succeeded
by Gretchen Soto

How would you feel if you couldn't read very well? Left out or embarrassed, of course. When I was in fifth grade, I was very much at a disadvantage. I had already been in five different schools, including two in Puerto Rico, in which I only studied in Spanish. Also, not every school teaches at the same level.

When I enrolled for school in the United States, the students in my new fifth grade class were already reading a novel titled, "Where the Red Fern Grows." After trying to catch up in the reading, I would get lost and not thoroughly understand what I was reading. My teacher, Mr. Gregory Hird, tried to help out as much as he could. He would read at a slow pace and define words he knew we wouldn't ask about to reflect on that we had just read or listened to.

After some time passed, I decided to talk to Mr. Hird in private. I told him I didn't want to read in front of the class because I couldn't read well and it would make me ashamed. When it was time for recess, he asked me to stay inside so we could read. We would go over words, and pronounce all kinds of words.

Many weeks passed, many reading sessions during recess, but it was all worth it. I was reading better, pronouncing my words better, and learning to understand the content I was reading. My test scores improved tremendously, and my interest in school and my desire to study all rose to a higher level. I had a "C" average in school, but once my reading had improved, I was an "A" student. Almost every-day before class started, Mr. Hird would ask how my reading was coming along. Now I can read a 200 page book in two to three days.

Mr. Hird has inspired me to go on and never stop trying. Mr. Hird took time out to help me out. There's a saying, "Where there is a problem, there is a solution." This is a very true statement and I guide myself with it. At the moment I am in the tenth grade and I must say that my reading has not declined since. Everyday I read part of a book, the Bible, or any other publication. I have not seen Mr. Hird for the past 5 years. I would like to say, "Thank you, Mr. Hird."

You Amaze Me

by Allison Speicher

Bill, junk mail, and—a letter? The return address is foreign. Instantly my head races with the endless possibilities of this envelope.

Upon opening that envelope, I went back in time to the years of curly blond pigtails and imploring green eyes that would drive most adults mad. The adult who facilitated my mental time travel on this day isn't like most. Where others saw nuisance, she saw brilliance, curiosity, a love of learning. She is my second grade teacher and my life teacher. If writers can be discovered, she discovered me. Miss C., to those who know and love her, coined the phrase, "Allison, you amaze me."

And now, it's time for me to give you a gift.... My first acrostic poem!

I attended a New York City public school, an understaffed, under budgeted school with too few books and too many students. More kids read below reading level than above it; more kids spoke a foreign tongue than understood English. Funding went for ESL and the inquisi-

tive overachiever could be left to grow lazy, while untapped potential atrophied. I could have been lost but I wasn't—because she always cared. Boredom was left undefined for me. I needed to explore worlds beyond my own. I may never understand it, but somehow Miss C. managed to increase literacy levels and keep me more than busy; I was learning. Somehow she always dreamed up that special something that only I could do, and time and time again, I was called to the front of the class to share my latest miraculous discovery. My "Rainforest Riddles" doubled her over with laughter; I was one of an elite minority of seven year olds who could name ten characteristics of the sloth. My joy was hers; we raised pennies that year and saved our very own acre of rainforest. Every day was a new adventure; I loved to go to school. Every new discovery was met by the same four words, the words that formed the foundation of who I am today: "Allison, you amaze me."

One day, we found it. More alluring than the rainforest, more intriguing than the sloth, we found my destiny together. I was a writer; my imagination and creative energies were funneled into something meaningful. A part of me was born that day that I will cherish for a lifetime. Our class threw Miss C. a surprise birthday party and I handed her my gift—my very first acrostic poem. At age seven, I had managed to rhyme the eighteen lines necessary to spell out Miss Castrogiovanni. I had arrived; I've never looked back.

It was this poem that bridged the gap of time and brought Miss C. back into my life. Years later, she found it, along with my new address. In her characteristic and "special person" nature, she wrote to me and the rest is history. Looking back at who I was and looking forward to who I'll be, only one line comes to mine: Miss Castrogiovanni, you amaze me.

The Lemonade Series

Don't Rush

by Shayla Stanley

The most influential teacher that I have ever had was my junior high band director. Her name is Cheryl Hopkins, and I learned more about music in the three years of being in her band than I'll learn for the rest of my life. She was more than a mere band director, though. She was a friend, she was a counselor, and she was a mentor. Most of her students, when passed into high school, continued to go back to J. T. Hutchison Junior High School at least once a week for updates on life. When the students could not make it back to her school, she would never fail to be at Lubbock High every week for the same purposes. The connection was easy, though, since her husband was the director at Lubbock High, also. The real influence was not in her curriculum, though. It was in the way she taught us, the way that she loved all of her students, and the way she told stories that made us realize that certain things should not be done. She wanted us to succeed in anything we did, even if it was not going to be music.

The memorable lesson she taught was the most personal for her— the death of her son, Jeffrey, who died in a car accident when he was seventeen. Since most of her students did not drive in junior high, she would tell us this story for the first lesson in driver's education. She always had pictures on hand when she saw someone, even a complete stranger, driving out of control, and Jeffrey's story to go along with it. She told us once on a Monday that she followed two high school students from an intersection where they almost hit her, all the way to the driver's house, stopped them from going inside, and told them her son's story and showed them pictures of the car that hit him. The students were very apologetic, which might have been a way to get Mrs. Hopkins out of their yard. But I still believe to this day that both the driver and the passenger were genuinely sorry about driving recklessly, and would never do it again in fear of either Mrs. Hopkins finding them again, or dying a death like her son did.

Forever Happy, Forever Grateful

by Karen Stufflebeam

The life of a teenager is hard enough, but additional stresses such as a miserable family life, few friendships, and low self-esteem can only make it worse. I was once in that place.

I've been in music programs since I was in the 5th grade, but it's only when I entered high school that I really started to enjoy music. My music teacher, Mr. John Neal, brought such energy and passion to music classes, that you couldn't help but love music. Not only was Mr. Neal a great teacher, but he was a great listener, too. When the bell rang at the end of the day, he didn't consider his job to be over…in my case, it was just beginning. I felt an immediate bond with Mr. Neal that allowed me to trust him, and share with him things that I just couldn't keep inside anymore. I was so emotionally beaten that I was making myself sick. With the help of Mr. Neal, I went to see the school social worker. But after our first appointment, she forgot about me, and we never met again. That's when Mr. Neal took over as my "therapist." I would tell him what happened at home the night before, what happened during that day at school, and how I was truly feeling deep down inside. I hit a point so low that I honestly thought I wouldn't make it through. I couldn't see the beauty of tomorrow or the joy of today. I only saw hopelessness with no escape. But, with the love and care I received from Mr. Neal, each day I grew stronger. He taught me to realize that I am "a treasure" and that I should never think any less of myself, no matter what anyone else said. He taught me to be happy with myself first…then and only then would I be able to be happy with other people. He taught me that there is goodness in every one and everything…and even though someone might be hurting me, I should forgive them, because grudges will only weight me down, and make my life worse.

I am now a senior in high school and I am the happiest I've every been in my entire life. Next year I will be heading off to college to be majoring in Psychology. Because of Mr. Neal, I want to help people the way he helped me. I want to let people know that there is someone who cares. One of the best things Mr. Neal gave me was confidence. He never doubted my abilities and always encouraged me to be the best I could be. Having someone right there with me, waiting to catch me if I fell, but always walking beside me to encourage me and help me along was the greatest feeling in the world. Without Mr. Neal, I would not be the person I am today.

Teaching With Love And Laughter
by Whitney Sugg

Have you ever been scared of something? Well, I have. In fact I am more or less a scaredy-cat. So last year when I walked into my first day of physics, I was more than a little afraid. Would I be able to complete the work? Was it going to be hard? How the heck was I going to make it through the year, I had no idea what physics was. Though at the same time I entered the classroom on my first day so did my savior, Mr. Janus. For the next mine months he would teach me that physics was not only an exciting subject, but that a little bit of love can go a long way.

For most people physics is no more than that image of Newton with the apple on his head, or Stephen Hawking, dictating another out-of-this-world theory. But to Mr. Janus and now myself, physics is a fun subject. I mean, how many people do you know that can figure out the speed a satellite travels around the earth? (O.K. besides your physics pals). Well let me tell you,

> If Rudolph decided to take a break on Christmas, I am sure that Santa will know who to call...

I can! And with the knowledge that I gained in taking Mr. Janus' class, I can dictate more than a couple of formulas. But that is not the point. The point is that Mr. Janus used fun to teach his class and allowed his students to expand their minds in whatever ways possible. He took such ideas as electricity and transferred it into the "Ted Bundy" lab, where we were able to take hot dogs and fry them with electricity, and even got the added bonus of eating them when we were done! We also played reindeer games, pulling one another, dressed as reindeer, around on a wood sleigh, and singing Christmas carols to our office staff, even to the principal and vice principal. He made the ideas that we learned fun, but also informational. In most classrooms that we pass through in our lives we ask ourselves, "When am I ever going to use this again?" But in Mr. Janus' class, the labs and information that we learned were directly applied to everyday life. I mean I may never pull a sleigh in my life, but if Rudolph decided to take a break on Christmas I am sure Santa will know who to call.

Mr. Janus has also demonstrated to me that a little love can go a long way. I am a member of the Republican Club, and living in a very Democratic state like California it can be more than a little hard to find a teacher that will look past a stereotype and back such a club. But he looked at us as another organization looking for some support, and not the neo-nazis that many assume us to be associated with. Through this club he has formed personal relationships with his students, always willing and ready to go to the demonstration or march on the Capitol. He also shows this same attitude in the class-room, winning every time the school newspaper takes a "favorite teacher" poll. He has shown me many a time that he is always willing to be there, through thick and thin, supporting, helping, and being an all around great guy.

When you walk into a classroom and see a longhaired, flip-flop-wearing ex-hippie, you would assume that it must be a parent that got lost, not an actual teacher, but you would be wrong. The state-ment, "Don't judge a book by its cover," fits Mr. Janus perfectly. While he may not appear to be professional, he is just the type of teacher that not only connects with his students and shows them love, but also makes them learn through exciting labs and lessons.

Mr. Cwodzinski
by Anna-Lisa Swank

Mr. Cwodzinski wasn't your normal American history teacher. In fact, he wasn't even normal. Even physically, at just over five feet, with a mop of curly black hair, large red-framed glasses, ratty tennis shoes, and a remarkable resemblance to the crazy scientist in "Honey, I Shrunk the Kids," he hardly blended in with fellow teachers. Needless to say, the enthusiastic shouting and frantic arm gestures during class only added to Mr. Cwodzinski's rather unique character. His uniqueness grew as class continued, for the more interesting the issue, the louder the volume and the more frenzied the motioning. If the topic was especially intriguing, a wild pacing in front of the blackboard ensued, punctuated by outrageous scribbling, lopsided figures, and half-finished sentences until, red in the face, Mr. Cwodzinski paused for air. When this occurred, the classroom remain frozen in anticipated silence for, most remarkable of all, we were held captive by his lessons.

I dare you to learn something new... even if it's a brand, new dance!

I use the word "remarkable" for I entered Mr. Cwodzinski's class rather wounded from my previous history course. The year before, the routine in history had been invariably the same. At the beginning of each class period, my teacher would clear his throat, pull at his tie, smooth down his comb-over, and recite the dreaded phrase, "Open your books to page...." I tried to make the best of the class, yet after a year of such treatment, I had developed a nervous twitch whenever hearing the word "history." So, although I received straight A's in the class, I was dying to take more out of history than good grades and ears still thudding from my teacher's perpetual monotone.

Thus, when Mr. Cwodzinski's class proved to be intellectually stimulating, my faith in the educational system, democracy, and the very fabric of America was restored. He immediately became a figure I looked up to (although not literally) for his unabashed passion for history was literally contagious. Without consciously realizing this, I became engrossed in the issues of our country's past. Yet his teaching went beyond facts.

I clearly remember Mr. Cwodzinski the day before our last final, defiantly standing in front of the class with a meter stick clenched in one hand (which he used to hit the blackboard whenever making a point) and a lopsided, but intelligent, grin on his face. He smacked the meter stick against the board for good measure—thwack!—and commanded, "Get out in the world and do something productive. Fail my final! I dare you!" Thwack! "Instead of cramming, go to a museum and enrich your life. Learn something new!" Thwack! "Don't let education get in the way of knowledge!"

Such impromptu decrees were often delivered in his classroom and, although I received an A on his final, I've remembered his message over the past few years. Sitting in his class as a wide-eyed sophomore, I learned that the best education surpasses textbooks and regular curriculums. Instead, it passes knowledge through energy and enthusiasm and creativity. So, although the image is rather comical, I'm completely serious when I declare that the epitome of the educational system—the very epitome of knowledge—is a curly haired, middle-aged man with large glasses and a dangerous meter stick.

Mr. Coward's Gumballs

by Leslie Tharp

I was valedictorian of my kindergarten class! I was bright and shiny and full of life. I was also a "social butterfly." This didn't seem like a bad thing until I got to first grade. There I had a teacher who thought that children should be seen, but not heard. She expected us to sit quietly and do our work, with no talking and no laughter. I often ended the day in the principal's office for "excessive talking and socializing." By the end of first grade, I was fed up with school. It wasn't any fun and I didn't want to go back. I was labeled a problem child. I will never forget you, Mrs. You Know Who You Are!

Wow, another gumball! I never knew learning could be so much fun!

Of course, my parents made me return to school in the fall. That year I got a man teacher—could my luck get any worse? Mr. Coward was retired military and had recently had a heart transplant. He told my parents that things would be different this year. He was so right! Mr. Coward had a gumball machine in his classroom. When you got an answer right or did well on a test or project or just had a good day, you got to get a gumball from the machine! You could only chew the gum in his classroom, though, not in the rest of the school! Our classroom was set up in "pods" and students were free to choose the activities that they enjoyed as long as they got the required work done first. There were animals in the classroom—one weekend I got to take the hermit crabs home! My parents were told that if I learned nothing else that year, I would learn to love to learn! Mr. Coward turned around my negative feelings for school with his innovative teaching methods and his genuine love for life. You see, he had been given a second chance at life and was now living life to the fullest, enjoying every day he was blessed with. As a fifth grader, I was Mr. Coward's classroom aid. As a middle schooler, I was a tutoring assistant for Mr. Coward. I would read to the 2nd graders and help work on their reading skills. Every year at open house, I went to see Mr. Coward and thank him for the gift he gave me. Last year I spoke at his funeral, along with hundreds of his former students who also came to honor him. I will graduate soon in the top 25% of my class. I have already been accepted to the college of my choice. I will take with me the love of learning I received from this wonderful teacher.

I will never forget you, Mr. Coward!

Teaching With Love And Laughter
by Mary Tolson

As an assistant in summer "B.E.A.R. Camp 2002" (Be Excited About Reading), I was introduced to the world of teaching through a special mentor. Ms. Berger offered my first up-close experience to the energy and patience required to teach a group of twenty 1st and 2nd grade children for 3-4 hours daily. She spent the week before camp designing learning centers and planning hands-on "bear activities." Everyday a new bear was introduced through literature, with related follow-up activities. The children were happily engaged in: 1) drawing pudding bears on paper plates; 2) reading with flashlights in the "bear cave;" 3) plunging shortening-covered hands in ice water to demonstrate a polar bear's need for blubber/fat; 4) using computers for "bear" research, bookmaking, creating poems, and T-shirt transfers; 5) writing to their own stuffed bears; 6) dancing to Chinese music with handmade "panda shakers;" 7) using gummy bears for math counters; and 8) having a Teddy Bear Tea with

Slip? I didn't slip! This is another way of doing the Panda Dance!

The Lemonade Series

parents. Ms. Berger enjoyed the days as much as her students did. She made "work" fun and gave the children choices when possible. She remained positive through all the spills, ripped papers, broken crayons, messy pudding hands, and lost macaroni noodles from the "shakers." When she misplaced things at times, she sent the children on an impromptu "treasure hunt" (how clever). I never heard her speak any negative remarks, and her passion for teaching was evident.

Ms. Berger had been teaching over 20 years; yet her enthusiasm reminded me of a new teacher. Once, she slipped while leading the panda dance. She laughed at herself (along with the children), picked herself up, wiggled her hips, and the dance went on! When a child said, "Ms. Berger, your stockings are falling," she just pulled them off and continued teaching. Mistakenly, she used all the gummy bears for her student's graphing activity (half were for the other teacher's class). The children had already eaten every last one, too! So I went to the nearest store, because "no child should go without." I never realized how much personal time and money a teacher invests in her students. When I thought of the materials needed for the numerous lessons, I began to appreciate her resourcefulness and generosity. Ms. Berger was prepared for anything. "From my Girl Scout days," she said. Her supply of tissues, soap, paper towels, plastic bags, even bath tissue was endless. "This is summer school and you can't count on getting what you need whenever you ask for it," she said. Ms. Berger always arrived at least an hour early and stayed to prepare for the next day. On the last day of B.E.A.R. Camp, every child had a family member or guardian participate! Many parents said they wanted to see why their children came home so excited.

This special teacher deserves recognition for her selflessness, and for teaching with love and laughter. She inspired me to focus on what was important—LOVE for all children.

The Greatest Teacher

by Katelyn Twichell

I have had many different teachers throughout my twelve year education. All have had some kind of impact on my life. However, my favorite teacher and the most significant and influential figure has been Mr. Hosea Stredic.

Mr. Stredic and I have had many disagreements throughout his teaching of government, religion, and almost anything you can imagine. We have had our private, dare I say, disciplinary talks as well as our public challenges. And yet, I always knew so clearly that he loved me, as a person, friend, and fellow Christian.

Mr. Stredic and I met on the first day that I came to Jesus Chapel High School. I was a shy, lonely junior and knew no one there. I walked into the Praise and Worship assembly auditorium. It was full, but I knew not a soul. Then, from across the auditorium, a well-built Black man waved me toward him. I was startled, and hesitated. He motioned to me again and I slowly started toward him. I still remember his soft, warm smile as he welcomed me to the new school and wished me a good first day. The good-natured torment began immediately. What classes was I in? What was it like to be the new girl? I was instantly comfortable with this person.

Mr. Stredic has taught me so many things since that first meeting and I appreciate them all. The most important thing he taught me was a self-confidence—confidence to speak out for what I believe in. I have learned to be true to myself, to never stop believing in me. I have learned to think before speaking and to listen to others' views and opinions and consider them. I learned how to make a point rather than to just argue.

One of Mr. Stredic's greatest qualities is that he does not require students to agree with him. Seldom have I been in a class where subjects can be discussed openly and from different points of view. Debates were sometimes heated, but he always treated us with respect.

Mr. Stredic will always be in my heart. I admire his personal strength and his seemingly unlimited love for his students. I respect his persistence and patience. Since meeting Mr. Stredic, I will never be the same.

> Every once in a while, remind yourself that "it's only money."

Dad's Lemonade Stand

Tips on Living with Love, Laughter and Lemonade!

A Lucrative Education
by Kate Vershov

The first day of AP Economics with Mr. Stange began with the following words: "This is not a democracy, this is a benevolent dictatorship. Then again, we are also a big, happy, slightly dysfunctional economics family." His class was special in the sense that all economic principles and graphical analyses were not the ends to our education experience. Instead, they were tools that we acquired. When he discussed economics, he made the graphs come alive as he gave them dimension through real-world applications and never failed to connect them to history, government, and even philosophy. We may have been studying oligopolies, but we were discussing the history of OPEC and how the war in Afghanistan was going to affect petroleum prices. When we learned about international trade, we debated the merits of George Bush's steel tariff. When we studied unemployment, we extrapolated what we knew about cyclical employment to predict how socialistic policies in some of the European nations affected the economy. Many of us would stay after class or come in during our lunch hours to finish the discussions we started.

He made me question the world around me more than I ever had before. Whatever the class dialogue may have been about, he always analyzed our arguments to their root assumptions and made us shed the blindfold of rhetoric and begin to synthesize information from a truly economic perspective. For instance, he played devil's advocate one day and announced, "The minimum wage is bad." Of course, I was shocked to hear this. But then he went on to question us on why this might be so. Finally, against all former intuition I had an idea. Perhaps when minimum wage is raised, companies are not able to staff as many people. For me, this was a revolutionary idea; this was a perspective I had never conceived.

Furthermore, Mr. Stange fostered individuality in his class. A student may give one answer, but he was never satisfied with only hearing one voice. He would turn to the other side of the room, point his finger at a person, and say, "What do you think?" For a man in his forties who is not afraid to wear a yellow bow tie, ride a bike to school every morning, or turn on "ska" in the classroom after school, we knew he was sincere in encouraging individualism.

Mr. Stange, however, was more than a great teacher, he inspired me. I actually began to read the Wall Street Journal, the full work of Adam Smith, and more contemporary economists such as Milton Friedman. I always knew I wanted to become a lawyer, but it was because of him that I decided to go into corporate law.

The most amazing thing of all was that Mr. Stange appeared to do everything effortlessly, even though I knew that he was a unique teacher and one who always accomplished more than he ever set out to do.

An Epiphany Of Empathy

by Judith Vick

Two white, Hershey Kiss-shaped blobs on the screen represented two communicating cells in the brain. The upper one spurted out red round balls, each like a water balloon filled with a chemical, to transport information to the second cell, lower on the screen. The computer program, displayed on a large, black monitor hanging precipitously from the classroom ceiling, simulated the communication between neurons in the brain that affect a person's mood and level of pleasure. My teacher pointed out that as the number of red balls changed, the bar on the pleasure meter on the screen rose or fell. By showing this much-simplified description of neural communication, my teacher, Mrs. Rapoport, made me realize the real and natural effect of chemicals in the brain.

As I transcribed the words from my teacher's mouth, I also transposed the representation on the screen to my own life. For the first time, I understood my father's lack of

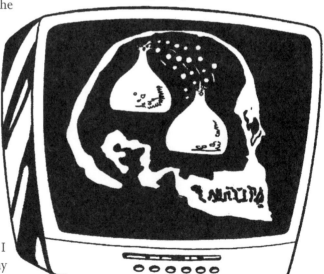

Now I get it!
I never looked at his
problems that way!

culpability for his mood swings. Though I had continuously been told he was not to blame for his manic-depression, Mrs. Rapoport made me truly understand his lack of control for the first time. I understood his inability to govern his moods, like a diabetic's inability to control his body's lack of production of insulin.

In that class, Mrs. Rapoport shaped how I saw my dad's mental illness. Viewing his fluctuation of moods—from confidence to depression, from energy to exhaustion, from dieting to overeating, from highs to lows—as the result of fluctuations of chemicals led me to understand him differently. This epiphany, in the apparent banality of a senior class, allowed me to love him. It allowed me to focus on his love for his family, his dedication to supporting us, and his desire to be a good parent, without being distracted by the malfunction of chemicals in his brain. That class led me to realize I resented the illness, and not him, even though it sometimes seems impossible to separate the two.

Mrs. Rapoport gave me an understanding I could never before grasp. She taught me how to view the world differently. She didn't give me one solution to one problem, help me thorough one difficult period in my life, or brighten just one bad day. By teaching my class neuroscience, without attaching stigma to any disease, Mrs. Rapoport taught us empathy. Knowing that so much is determined by the inner workings of the brain, I have been able to view the world with more compassion, to understand people, their personalities, and their actions better. I know that other people in my class felt the same way. Mrs. Rapoport changed our mindsets, expanding the window through which we see the world.

One Little Speech

by Candace Vickers

There's been an accident. These four words that forced themselves reluctantly from my mother's lips would haunt me for the rest of my life and stand as a monument to one of life's greatest tragedies: The loss of a parent.

The next few days were lost in a haze of confusion and exhaustion. Convinced that there were more important things to be dealt with, I set aside my grief and shock, to be absorbed when there was time to do so. I found consolation only in the distance I placed between myself and what had happened.

Beginning to feel the burden of my own isolation, I found myself wanting to return to the one place I knew had not changed, school.

The chaos of a gym filled with children waiting to begin class instantly engulfed me and the familiarity settled my anxious mind. Ironically, it was this roar of children's excited voices that was the most calming thing I had heard in what seemed like years.

In time, our teacher arrived, Mrs. Skiles. She was a delightfully cheerful woman who hardly seemed like a teacher at all, but rather, a motherly companion. She gingerly gestured at me to join her where she stood. "Candi, I just want you to know that if you need anything, I'm here."

Class turned out to be more difficult than anticipated. I alternated between fidgeting and dazing. I simply could not escape the overwhelming thoughts regarding the frivolity of the subject matter. Somehow, long division no longer seemed pertinent in any way.

As the class dismissed for lunch, I was again called to the side of the teacher. "You haven't been your usual self today, hon. Are you okay?"

I sighed and commenced to tell her the reason for my restlessness.

All the while, she listened intently. When I was done, she waited a moment before saying, "The truth is, Candi, you can't expect to go back to who you were before. You have encountered and dealt with

The Lemonade Series

one of the harshest things life has to offer. You were forced to develop a certain level of maturity in order to cope. However, that maturity also comes with a frustration with the mundane details of life. There will be times when things you used to like seem frivolous and your peers seem incredibly immature but you must be patient with them. And when you start to feel that the classes and material you must learn is irrelevant, simply remember that your end goal is to continually challenge yourself to do better."

I mulled over what she had said and the more I did, the more sense it made. I'm a senior in high school now and, seven years after it was made, her little speech has never failed me. As college and life stand before me as an ominous mountain, I hold it a little closer and trudge on, always the dream that lies just on the other side.

> It's always OK to feel another's pain, but it's never OK to postpone joy.

Dad's Lemonade Stand

Tips on Living with Love, Laughter and Lemonade!

The Magister

by Aaron Warchal

An educational role model is a person who lives their life according to high moral standards and displays selfless behavior when interacting with other people. The person who most exemplifies this life style is my Latin teacher, Mr. Michael Kitsock.

Better known to his students as, "The Magister," (Latin term for teacher) Mr. Kitsock is a master of student motivation. Whether he is performing his famous pen tricks, singing a melody to aid in memory formation or just being his charismatic self, Magister works hard at holding our attention. It's no fluke that over half of incoming sophomores register for Latin. It's not the course material that attracts potential students—it's the reputation of the teacher.

Mr. Kitsock grew up surrounded by poverty. Because he understands the burdens of the poor, his Latin Club annually collects canned food for the local shelters. Last year, we tipped the 3,000 can mark. He constantly reminds us of the value of continued education and self sacrifice.

Magister has been a volunteer firefighter and EMT since 1969. He is currently the President of his community's Historical Fire Society and runs the local fire museum. He is married and spends much time raising his autistic son, James, in a loving and patient environment.

He is a true American Hero and role model for his students. With little fanfare, he sacrifices each day to provide a better atmosphere for the lives he touches. As I venture into the teacher preparation program at the college level, I plan to emulate the "Magister" on both a personal and professional basis.

My Teacher; My Savior

by Jessica Rose Weiner

I battled severe depression in silence, for a long time, seriously contemplating suicide as a last resort—an immediate solution to all of my problems and pain. Initially I was absolutely petrified of confessing my internal struggles to anyone; I guess I saw this as a weakness. As a rule I always conceal my feelings so as not to place myself in a situation where I am susceptible to more hurt and pain. However, this particular viewpoint gets me into more trouble with myself, because all the unhappiness just builds up until I ultimately reach the breaking point, the point where I lash out at others and myself. That precise "doomsday" silently but obviously crept up on me sometime last year during English class. I received permission to leave the class and I literally ran, with tears streaming down my face, to Laurie Turner's room. I knew she was teaching a class that period, but I desperately had to talk to someone and she is the only teacher I have formed a significant relationship with. I knew she would understand and point me in the right direction.

There I sat, crumpled in a little wailing ball, outside her door. She appeared in front of me after a while, and persuaded me to see an on-site counselor; she actually escorted me into the office and once I felt secure, returned to her eager students. The on-site counselors called an off-site crisis counselor, and my situation continued from there. Not to get into every single detail of my traumatic episode, but I can honestly say that my teacher was ultimately my savior. She saw through my tough exterior and wanted to assist me in calming my rough interior; she actually cared enough about one of her students to take time out of her life and help me focus on mine.

Throughout my years in high school, I have never encountered such a great teacher. Laurie Turner is clearly passionate about the subject she teaches and, in effect, learning turns into an enjoyable experience; she is also passionate about helping her students. She takes the time and energy to consult with each student, motivates and encourages them to pursue anything they desire. She modifies the many obstacles in high school to make them appear to be minimal and bearable; she will hold our hand along the way if we are scared, but separates herself enough so you can grow on your own. Fremont High School is better because of Laurie Turner, and if I did not meet her I know I would be far worse off. Instead of thinking of teachers as dictating, unmerciful tyrants, think of them as life's greatest motivators.

"Dukey"

by Ashley Wetherell

Throughout my high school journey at Wahconah Regional, there have been lessons to be learned. The most important lesson I have learned is to live life to its fullest and to face my fears. This lesson comes from an amazing freshman English teacher by the name of Mr. James Duquette.

Whether it's Thomas Jefferson, Or me...as Dukey says, "Ride your tigers!"

Every day in the classroom, Mr. James Duquette, or Dukey, as most everyone called him, would give us "PR's" (Latin prefixes) and "News Voc" to prepare us for our future inside and outside Wahconah. He would also tell his students to live their lives by a special code: "If you live your life with Z, G, AV, IV, F and L, you will lead a wonderful life." These letters stood for: Zest, Gusto, Animal Vigor, Intellectual Vigor, Fun and Love. This was a quote borrowed from one of his favorite novels, *Dandelion Wine*. Living by these words, it was not unusual to see Dukey, at the age of 59, out running every day. Another favorite saying of his was, "Ride your tigers," which came from Thomas Jefferson's quote, "We must ride our tigers, or they will surely eat us." While Jefferson's quote refers to U.S. politics and government, James Duquette encouraged us to face the "tigers" that everyday life had to offer whether it was a test in his classroom, a tough opponent on the basketball court, or a problem in our personal lives. He meant for us, his students, to face life head-on and accept the challenges we constantly meet.

Dukey showed me that reading is enjoyable, even though I struggled in this subject. There were many nights I devoted two hours to just my English homework. My mom spent countless hours with me reading the classics that are assigned to freshman English. In spite of my struggle during that year, I can honestly say I enjoyed his class more than any other I have ever taken. With his special lessons and codes, he also showed me how to succeed in basketball. I worked hard to improve my game and overcome the obstacles I encountered on the court.

On an April day in the year 2002, Mr. James Duquette died from a six-month battle with cancer. Even though he struggled with this illness, he found ways to keep a positive attitude. At his funeral, hundreds of people came to pay their respects, including his friends and family as well as past and present students. People will never forget Mr. Duquette and the special person he was; he has touched the lives of almost everyone in our small community.

Because of this man, many of his former students have gone into the career of Education. He made reading and learning fun and school a great place to be. He taught me life lessons that will stay with me forever. Even though I wasn't one of his top students, I have never met a teacher quite like Mr. James Duquette. Thanks to Dukey, I am learning to "ride my tigers."

Lemon Jelly
by Bridget Williams

I remember my first day of middle school like it was yesterday. The eighth graders looked so big. The hallways wound endlessly. The teachers were not as friendly looking as the teachers in elementary school. And the classes were not as fun.

All day long I did problems that everyone was to do the exact same way. In gym we all had to move together. In speech we all had to speak together. My last class of the day was Creative Writing. I don't know how I managed to hang in there until then. Relief ran through my eleven-year-old body like a tidal wave when I first saw the curly haired women behind the desk. She introduced herself as Mrs. Brandel and gave us our first assignment. On the white board (they were green in elementary school) she wrote, "When life hands you lemons make..." and asked us to write a story completing the sentence. I could think only of the lemon jelly my grandmother used to make when I'd come visit her. I was eleven. I didn't know better. But I soon learned as my classmates went around the room reading their stories that "lemonade" was the correct answer.

When it was my turn, I sunk in my chair and shyly read what I had conjured up about my grandmother's lemon jelly. They laughed at me. Kids can be so cruel. But Mrs. Brandel praised me for not being like everybody else. She told me originality is a very respectable trait. I was always encouraged by her to be creative and I feel I would not be where I am today had I not.

I have been working in the field of animation; one that constantly demands new and creative ideas. Thank you, Mrs. Brandel.

She said, 'be yourself!'.... But who knew it would lead to this!

Sweetener Of My Lemonade
by Liynaa'a Willoughby

When someone enters your life and changes your entire perspective of the world, it makes life worth while. I never believed that in the short term of five months, one man could fill my heart with the treasures of a lifetime: uplifted hopes, positive outlooks, and the endurance to believe that even the most impossible dreams can come true, even for a disbeliever like me.

He once said that teaching is a joy for him; describing his students as one big family, I could tell that this man was touched by God. His ability to transform the worst situation into a positive opportunity continues to amaze me. I can only hope that I can impact someone's life with at least a fraction of the faith that he instilled in mine.

My day always seemed to be like a sour glass of lemonade. My face was all puckered up until I reached my third class of the day, African American History. Whether I needed a smile, joke, or a simple pat on the back, he was there. I could never leave his classroom without a smile. In some mysterious way, he added a bag of sugar so that the remainder of my lemonade could be as sweet as can be. I still can't figure out how he did it!

To me, life is like riding a bicycle. Everyone has their own hills to pedal over, but it seemed as if mine were too steep to conquer. I always knew that I wanted to excel in life, but I never had the extra push that I needed to get to the top of my hill, nor did I know how to get there. I want to thank Mr. Rodney Wilds for pushing me as hard as he possibly could. Because of your influence in my life, I am determined to tackle the hills of impossibility, and make it to the top of each one standing in my way. His friendly embrace will forever be anchored in my heart. Mr. Wilds, you are a blessing on Earth. Thanks for the memories and chance of a lifetime.

The Lemonade Series

Name, Dates, And Friendship

by David Wonpu

It was one of those moments that I used to think only happened in teen movies. The actor would turn away from the camera and squeeze out a Visine tear to the sounds of a pop-rock band's biggest hit. This time, however, there was no clever soundtrack. I rolled out of bed, did my morning routine that I've perfected through the years, drove to school, and felt like I was going to die. It hit me out of nowhere, and put me in so much pain that could feel it in every single pore. I hated myself. I'm sure that there was some conscious part of me that knew what a fluke I was. I was a senior, I had met a girl, and I had a job. But the increasing cloudiness in my eyes told me a different story.

I didn't know who to talk to. Among my friends, I was always the counselor, not the counseled. My parents were both at work. It seemed like I had no one.

Then I remembered my junior year History teacher. Mr. Nielson not only had the most thought-provoking mind I've ever been in the presence of, he was also a friend. There was always something so good about him, as if he could uncover the truth behind even the most complicated of teenage ramblings.

I walked to his class, and, as always, the door was open. "Hey Mr. Nielson," I said. "Hi Dave, good to see you again." "Hey Mr. Nielson, can I talk to you?" "Sure."

I asked how the year was going so far, as well as his plans for next year. They were the kinds of casual questions any nervous teenager asked before he's about to put his hidden emotions on the line.

And then it all came out. I told him about all of the uncertainties and insecurities that I've carried around for the last four years. I was scared of the real world. He assured me that I was more than capable of handling it. I expressed the frustration I felt over growing up Chinese and American at the same time. He told me that, in time, I would discover my place in the world. But most of all, I told him my real fear: that no one ever noticed me. "If I died," I asked him, "who would miss me?" "More people than you think," he said. "The people that you yourself don't notice."

I thanked him and we hugged in the kind of way I would've embraced the older brother I never had. I walked out of his class and into a new day. What was I to be sad about again?

The Unforgettable Mr. Ron Carr

by Adam Zaremba

Throughout my four years in high school, I have gone trough many teachers that have taught me lessons and disciplined me to be the best in my field. Yet one teacher stands out above the rest. In my wonderful school of Riverview High School, we have distinguished groups of individuals that consist of accelerated learning and higher level classes above the normal: the International Baccalaureate (IB) program. I have been in this program for four years and have finally completed it with 36 other colleagues, and all of us have received lectures and various lessons from a highly influential individual, Mr. Ron Carr.

Mr. Carr was my teacher when I took a class called, The Theory of Knowledge (TOK), where we learned about knowledge issues and ways of thinking. The class taught me about morals in life and how to deal with others in certain situations as well as making just decisions. Why would this class make me feel that Mr. Carr was such a fantastic individual? My reasoning is simple; it's not just this class. Mr. Carr has been working at our school for 35 years now. He has served as an athletic coach for numerous sports, a speech and debate coach (recognized around the nation for his expertise), English teacher, IB coordinator, and as a mentor and tutor in many other subjects. Obviously, I see Mr. Carr as a man who has not only accomplished what many could not accomplish in a lifetime, but also earned the job satisfaction through his teaching that many do not get a chance to experience. Many of my teachers that have been teaching for years had Mr. Carr as a teacher when they were students, which brings an even more spiritual bond to the significance of Mr. Carr and his teaching.

Mr. Carr has not only served as my teacher, but he also became a mentor of mine during specific assignments in school and for the IB program by extracting my best skills and making me put them to good use. He has changed my personality from a somewhat disrespectful and irresponsible student to a sophisticated and hardworking individual who will soon pursue a career in medicine. If I did not have a teacher like Mr. Carr, who knows what would have become of me, as well as my other fellow students that were permanently changed through his lessons and moral discussions.

What truly brings a tear to my eye is that I am leaving school this summer to continue life as a college student, and Mr. Carr is leaving with his hard-earned retirement. With his 35 years of teaching and motivating students into becoming all that they can be, Mr. Carr will surely never be forgotten by the staff and students at Riverview High School, always remembered for his hard work, humor, determination and care for others and their lives. Goodbye Mr. Carr, I hope we meet again sometime. "That would be nice...that would be really nice."

The Lemonade Series

English As A Second Language
by Elena Zeltser

Each person has his individual path in life, with its detours and directions. However, there are people in each of our lives who direct us, help us, and encourage us. I would like to talk about such a person in my life. When my family immigrated to the United States three years ago, I spoke practically no English. Entering high school as a freshman, I was put in the English as a Second Language class, and met the person who would not only teach English, but would direct my interests, help me establish myself in the new school, and encourage me in everything I did—my ESL teacher, Mrs. Meany.

The help that I received from my teacher with English was simply tremendous. In a very short time of studying the language with Mrs. Meany I could speak English, not perfectly, but understandably. From the very beginning, as I came to the class each day, she would listen to my speaking and try to understand each word that I was saying. I am sure that it was not easy for a person to understand me. My

> **When I sing, my accent goes away....**
> **And opens my life to new friends!**

teacher's listening gave me great encouragement and brought my self-esteem to a much higher level.

As I learned to speak English, my ESL teacher learned more about me. One thing that Mrs. Meany found out was my great interest in music. In Russia, my native country, I had studied violin and music theory for eight years in Moscow's specialized music school. I also enjoyed singing. Upon finding that out, Mrs. Meany told me about the music department in the school. She explained to me all about choral classes and band. She was the one who encouraged me to join the concert choir. Mrs. Meany also encouraged me to join the Interact club, a service club for all the foreign students in our school and also for anybody else who wanted to meet new friends.

Three years later, not only am I no longer in the ESL program, but now I am taking AP English, and my English has improved so much that I was chosen to read announcements on our school public address system. I enjoy belonging to many different clubs, especially the Speech and Debate club, in which I am the President, Chamber Choir, The Academic Challenge team, and the Math Honor Society. My best friends are those who I met in these clubs.

Without her, my ESL teacher, I would never have found myself in the situation I am presently in: confident, surrounded by friends and ready for my next step in life, college. I hope there will be many more students for Mrs. Meany to direct, help, and encourage, just like she did with me.

The Path
by Joyce Zhang

Ninja Turtles: the first impression I had of my favorite teacher. As a child, I was obsessed with them. Seeing them on her wall immediately drew me to her. Mrs. King, or Magistra Rex as we called her while learning Latin, was exceptional. I had the privilege of having her as a teacher for a GT program at my elementary school in Texas from third to sixth grade.

While other teachers were usually soft-spoken, she was loud. Where they had even handwriting, hers was wild. They had tidy desks. You could hardly see the wood on her cluttered desk, and we loved her for it. As I learned from her, originality is what distinguishes a person. We learned a vast array of knowledge with Mrs. King, from Roman culture and only speaking in Latin, to participating in Future Problem Solving and competing at the state level, to learning poetry. The message she constantly emphasized was to be creative and original. She instilled in me a sense of a greater purpose, to strive for my goals. Others may preach modesty, but she taught us that we were special and should always strive to excel.

I remember the activities and games in that class. Some would consist of drawing and elaborating upon a simple shape and creating something completely unique from it, or thinking of objects that were white and seeing how many original objects someone could come up with that nobody else in the class had. As a child, I took the message of being my own unique person to heart, without quite realizing why. When picking topics for class, I would always pick the hardest topic, the one almost nobody else would choose. Even for Halloween, I disliked being a witch, because every girl dresses as one at one point. I sometimes marvel how, at such a young age, I was already being my own person. Now, we learn more complex terms such as Transendentalism and non-conformity, but at the root, the ideals are still the same. Mrs. King taught me to ignore the bandwagon. It is said that our personalities are established by the age of eleven. I am thankful to her that I learned of individuality before that age.

In an increasingly competitive world, the innovative and novel stand out while the rest blend and fade into the background. To be accepted into the college of one's choice, to attain a special job, to achieve recognition, one must be better than the rest. Mrs. King taught me how to use the wonderful tool I possess, called the mind, to think for myself and not allow the thoughts of others to govern. She changed my entire outlook on the world at a time when I was unable to comprehend how much she had opened the world for me. When jogging through the woods of life, I may come to a fork in the road, but thanks to her, I will know to take the path less traveled. Thank you, Mrs. King!

End each day with your thoughts filled with thanks.

Dad's Lemonade Stand

Tips on Living with Love, Laughter and Lemonade!

Contributing Authors

Abbott, Samara—Patrick Henry High School, Roanoke VA
Andrade, Skye—Waimea High School, Lawai, HI
Angiuli, Anthony—Cardinal Newman High School, West Palm Beach, FL
Arnold, Laura—Normal Community West High School, Normal, IL
Arquines, Alea—Sammamish High School, Bellevue, WA
Artz, Josh—Germantown High School, Memphis, TN
Bansal, Rahul—Cypress Falls High School, Houston, TX
Beck, Kellie—South Lake High School, Clermont, FL
Blosser, Kelly—Eagle's Landing High School, Mc Donough, GA
Bronstein, Nadya—Ladue Horton Watkins, St. Louis, MO
Brooks, Kayla—Henrietta, TX
Bryant, Joseph—Philadelphia, PA
Bryant, Katie—Home Schooled, Rogers, AR
Butcher, John—Bandera High School, Pipe Creek, TX
Cable, David—Peculiar, MO
Church, Miranda—Delaware Valley Regional High School, Bloomsbury, NJ
Cleveland, Crystal—Auburndale High School, Auburndale, FL
Clippinger, Becci—Southwestern Randolph High School, Denton, NC
Cohen, Camille—Coral Reef High School, Miami, FL
Collier, Jessica—Wayne Central High School, Walworth, NY
Connolly, Lauren—Boces Cultural Arts Center, Smithtown, NY
Connor, Kyndra—Green River, WY
Corriveau, Bethany—City High School, Grand Rapids, MI
Dimanche, Claudia—William H. Turner Technical Sr. Arts High School, North Miami, FL
Dozier, Katherine—Cocoa Beach Jr/Sr High School, Merritt Island, FL
Eskridge, Frankie—Howard D. Woodson High School, Washington, DC
Evans, Debra—Northampton Sr. High School, Bethlehem, PA
Flaherty, Britt—Yuba City High School, Yuba City, CA
Ford, Kristen—Carlsbad High School, Carlsbad, CA
French, Blake—Mason High School, Mason, MI
Gage, Lauren—East Providence High School, East Providence, RI
Glagola, Caroline—F. W. Buchholz High School, Gainesville, FL
Goracke, Megan—Prior Lake High School, Prior Lake, MN
Greco, James—Hesperia, CA
Grove, Aaron—City High School, Iowa City, IA
Harter, Ashley—Conrad Weiser High School, Wernersville, PA
Havens, Megan—Clermont Northeastern High School, Batavia, OH
Henrich, Rachel—Mound Westonka High School, Mound, MN
Hogan, Kelli—Grosse Pointe South High School, Grosse Pointe Park, MI
Hughes, Victoria—Palm Harbor University High, Oldsmar, FL
Hurt, Michael—Northport High School, East Northport, NY
Iwanabe, Kelly—Huntington Beach, CA
Jefferis, Danielle—Central High School, Grand Junction, CO
Jetton, Jamie—Oak Ridge High School, Spring, TX
Kellman, Corie—Chelsea High School, Gregory, MI
Kidd, Aimee—Westminster High School, Westminster, ND

Kloehn, Kathryn—Las Lomas High School, Walnut Creek, CA
Knutson, Melissa—Berlin High School, Berlin, WI
Lassabe, Ryan—Lutheran High School, Metairie, LA
Lawhon, Catherine—West Florence High School, Florence, SC
Liptak, Jessica—Carmel High School, Wauconda, IL
Maddock, C. Keane—Frankfort Senior High School, Frankfort, IN
Marcoe, Erin—Eagle, ID
Marquardt, Barry—Kaukauna High School, Appleton, WI
Marrero, Melissa—Monte Vista High School, Alamo, CA
Martin, Lashanna—Bishop Hannan High School, Scranton, PA
Matthews, Shaday—Benjamin E. Mays High School, Atlanta, GA
McIlwain, Elizabeth—Tuscaloosa County High School, Tuscaloosa, AL
Mercedes, Jasmin—Rosa Parks High School, Paterson, NJ
Methven, Tanya—Clackamas High School, Portland, OR
Minkow, Megan—Trinity Preparatory School, Winter Park, FL
Molino, Christina—A&M Consolidated High School, College Station, TX
Monrian, Grace—Bakersfield, CA
Mun, Cherry—Irvington High School, Fremont, CA
Oghor, Doris—Lamar Consolidated High School, Sugar Land, TX
Olshever, Erin—Great Neck South High School, Lake Success, NY
Parker, Roxanne—Moravia, IA
Potter, Betsy—Traverse City, MI
Pouliot, Eric—Southbridge, MA
Rainey, Jenni—Monticello, IL
Reeder, Jessica—Weber High School, Ogden, UT
Roth, Cynthia—Valley Stream Jr/Sr High School, Valley Stream, NY
San Agustin, Leah—Whittier Christian School, La Habra, CA
Semple, Kathryn—Tempe, AZ
Snyder, Misty—Tyrone Area High School, Tyrone, PA
Soto, Gretchen—Avon Park High School, Avon Park, FL
Speicher, Allison—W.C. Mepham High School, North Bellmore, NY
Stanley, Shayla—Lubbock High School, Lubbock, TX
Stufflebeam, Karen—Litchfield, ME
Sugg, Whitney—Newcastle, CA
Swank, Anna-Lisa—Principia Upper School, Ballwin, MO
Tharp, Leslie—San Antonio, TX
Tolson, Mary Elizabeth—Chesapeake, VA
Twichell, Katelyn—Jesus Chapel School, El Paso, TX
Vershov, Kate—Towson High School, Owings Mills, MD
Vick, Judith—Beth Tfiloh Dahan Community High School, Baltimore, MD
Vickers, Candace—Mingus Union High School, Cottonwood, AZ
Warchal, Aaron—Reading, PA
Weiner, Jessica Rose—Fremont High School, Sunnyvale, CA
Wetherell, Ashley—Wahconah Regional High School, Dalton, MA
Williams, Bridget—Rogers High School, Wyoming, MI
Willoughby, Liynaa'a—Page High School, Greensboro, NC
Wonpu, David—Community College High School-East, North Las Vegas, NV
Zaremba, Adam—Riverview High School, Sarasota, Fl
Zeltser, Elena—Matawan Regional High School, Matawan, NJ
Zhang, Joyce—International Academy, West Bloomfield, MI

Call, Email or Visit
TODAY
to order more copies of this book
at $12.95 per copy
Teaching with Love, Laughter & Lemonade
Student & teacher 20% discount available—
enter Promo Code **EDUCATOR** or **STUDENT**.

Here's How To Order:

Visit: www.DadsLemonadeStand.com
to order books & additional products.
Email: Paul@DadsLemonadeStand.com
Call: 1-800-808-2315

The Lemonade Series

Also Presents
Products to Promote
A Sweeter Life!

A Daddy's World by Paul S. Bodner   **Special Price**
The first book in The Lemonade Series.   **$9.95**
A Collection of stories that will change,   (Reg. $17.77)
inspire, and ultimately sweeten your life.

A Daddy's World Audio Book   **Special Price**
A double CD recording of **A Daddy's World.**   **$9.95**
Enjoy this wonderful collection of stories   (Reg. $17.77)
narrated by Paul S. Bodner.

10 Tips To Getting A Grip
On Living With Love & Laughter   **Special Price**
This clever jar opener with inspirational   **$2.00**
messages from Dad's Lemonade Stand offers   **6 for $10.00**
tips you'll hold on to every day!